# How to Build Shlaer-Mellor Object Models

ANDREWS AND LEVENTHAL   Fusion: Integrating IE, CASE, and JAD
ANDREWS AND STALICK   Business Reengineering: The Survival Guide
AUGUST   Joint Application Design
BODDIE   The Information Asset: Rational DP Funding and Other Radical Notions
BOULDIN   Agents of Change: Managing the Introduction of Automated Tools
BRILL   Building Controls into Structured Systems
COAD AND NICOLA   Object-Oriented Programming
COAD AND YOURDON   Object-Oriented Analysis, 2/E
COAD AND YOURDON   Object-Oriented Design
COAD WITH NORTH AND MAYFIELD   Object Models: Strategies, Patterns,
     and Applications
CONNELL AND SHAFER   Object-Oriented Rapid Prototyping
CONNELL AND SHAFER   Structured Rapid Prototyping
CONSTANTINE   Constantine on Peopleware
CONSTANTINE AND YOURDON   Structured Design
CRAWFORD   Advancing Business Concepts in a JAD Workshop Setting
DEGRACE AND STAHL   The Olduvai Imperative: CASE and the State of Software
     Engineering Practice
DEGRACE AND STAHL   Wicked Problems, Righteous Solutions
DEMARCO   Controlling Software Projects
DEMARCO   Structured Analysis and System Specification
EMBLEY, KURTZ, AND WOODFIELD   Object-Oriented Systems Analysis
FOURNIER   Practical Guide to Structured System Development and Maintenance
GARMUS AND HERRON   Measuring the Software Process: A Practical Guide
     to Functional Measurements
GLASS   Software Conflict: Essays on the Art and Science of Software Engineering
JONES   Assessment and Control of Software Risks
KING   Project Management Made Simple
LARSON   Interactive Software: Tools for Building Interactive User Interfaces
MCMENAMIN AND PALMER   Essential System Design
MOSLEY   The Handbook of MIS Application Software Testing
PAGE-JONES   Practical Guide to Structured Systems Design, 2/E
PINSON   Designing Screen Interfaces in C
PUTNAM AND MYERS   Measures for Excellence: Reliable Software on Time
     within Budget
RIPPS   An Implementation Guide to Real-Time Programming
RODGERS   ORACLE®: A Database Developer's Guide
RODGERS   UNIX®: Database Management Systems
SHLAER AND MELLOR   Object Lifecycles: Modeling the World in States
SHLAER AND MELLOR   Object-Oriented Systems Analysis: Modeling the World in Data
STARR   How to Build Shlaer-Mellor Object Models
THOMSETT   Third Wave Project Management
WANG (ed.)   Information Technology in Action
WARD   System Development Without Pain
WARD AND MELLOR   Structured Development for Real-Time Systems
YOURDON   Decline and Fall of the American Programmer
YOURDON   Managing the Structured Techniques, 4/E
YOURDON   Managing the System Life-Cycle, 2/E
YOURDON   Modern Structured Analysis
YOURDON   Object-Oriented Systems Design
YOURDON   Rise and Resurrection of the American Programmer
YOURDON   Structured Walkthroughs, 4/E
YOURDON   Techniques of Program Structure and Design
YOURDON AND ARGILA   Case Studies in Object-Oriented Analysis and Design
YOURDON, WHITEHEAD, THOMANN, OPPEL, AND NEVERMANN   Mainstream
     Objects: An Analysis and Design Approach for Business
YOURDON INC.   YOURDON™ Systems Method: Model-Driven Systems Development

# How to Build

## Shlaer-Mellor

# Object Models

### Leon Starr

### Model Integration, Inc.

*For book and bookstore information*

http://www.prenhall.com

**YOURDON PRESS**
**Prentice Hall Building**
**Upper Saddle River, New Jersey 07458**

Library of Congress Cataloging-in-Publication Data

Starr, Leon.
   How to build Shlaer-Mellor object models / Leon Starr.
      p.  cm. -- (Yourdon Press computing series)
   Includes index.
   ISBN 0-13-207663-2
   1. Object-oriented programming (Computer science) 2.System analysis.  I. Title.  II. Series
   QA76.64.S718   1996
   005.1'2--dc20                               96-19450
                                              CIP

Editorial/production supervision: *Joanne Anzalone*
Manufacturing manager: *Alexis R. Heydt*
Acquisitions editor: *Paul Becker*
Editorial assistant: *Maureen Diana*
Cover design director: *Jerry Votta*

Published  by Prentice Hall PTR
Prentice-Hall, Inc.
A Simon & Schuster Company
Upper Saddle River, New Jersey 07458

The publisher offers discounts on this book when ordered in bulk quantities.
For more information, contact:
Corporate Sales Department
Prentice Hall PTR
1 Lake Street
Upper Saddle River, NJ 07458

Phone: 800-382-3419, Fax: 201-236-7141
E-mail: corpsales@prenhall.com

Printed in the United States of America
10 9 8 7 6 5 4 3 2 1

**ISBN 0-13-207663-2**

Prentice-Hall International (UK) Limited, *London*
Prentice-Hall of Australia Pty. Limited, *Sydney*
Prentice-Hall Canada Inc., *Toronto*
Prentice-Hall Hispanoamericana, S.A., *Mexico*
Prentice-Hall of India Private Limited, *New Delhi*
Prentice-Hall of Japan, Inc., *Tokyo*
Simon & Schuster Asia Pte. Ltd., *Singapore*
Editora Prentice-Hall do Brasil, Ltda., *Rio de Janeiro*

*To mom and dad*

# Contents

## 7   Advanced supertype relationships 115

# HOW TO BUILD USEFUL MODELS

## 12   How to write relationship descriptions 199

# MODEL PATTERNS

## 13   Is zero-one-many specific enough? 209

# 14 Reflexive patterns 215

# 15 Network patterns 223

## 16 Linear patterns 237

## 17 Tree patterns 261

# Foreword

Leon Starr's book is a practical guide. It starts from the beginning by explaining the essentials of the method, and it illustrates the implications of these essentials as they apply in practice. The book contains a wealth of examples drawn from real-world experience, and these examples are used to make concrete the abstractions you encounter in real projects. The book tells you - and *shows* you - how to build useful models quickly. There is a good deal of excellent advice on how to manage your own analysis activities to get the most useful models for the least work.

But the heart of the book is the illustration of how to think about a problem by extracting its essential nature. Consider the problems of modeling a sheet with an image on each side or a pipe length separated by a valve. These seemingly trivial problems are more difficult than they appear because they are highly constrained. This book leads you through the choices you must make so that the concept of "two-sidedness" stands exposed. And you acquire an understanding of the analysis thinking process that led to it.

A glance through the book will show that it focuses on object information modeling. There are two reasons for this. First, the selection of abstractions is the most important step in the method, and these abstractions constitute the framework around which everything else is built. Second, if you get the object information model right, the state models become radically simpler. Mr. Starr knows this from experience: he has built Shlaer-Mellor OOA models for a very wide variety of applications and learned the hard way that the object information model is key.

Leon began work on Shlaer-Mellor models with us at Project Technology, Inc., in 1985. This was before, as he likes to say, his "warranty ran out." It was fun to work with Leon then, and it is now. You will see Leon's twisted sense of humor all over these pages, sometimes belying the depth of his experience. Don't let it fool you. Read the book, learn from it, and - most of all - enjoy it.

Sally Shlaer
Stephen J. Mellor

Berkeley, California

# Author's preface

This book is a collection of models, modeling tips, and analysis techniques that have worked for me (and my colleagues) on real projects. It conveys some of the experience that I have gained in 10 years of building Shlaer-Mellor models. I have written this book for those of you who have had an introduction to the Shlaer-Mellor method through some combination of courses and books. I presume that you are either about to start applying the method on your project or that you have been building Shlaer-Mellor models for a year or two. This text is geared toward those of you who do the hard work of boiling down application requirements, formalizing these requirements into fully detailed models and ,getting those models translated into working software.

This book is not a complete statement or grammar of the Shlaer-Mellor modeling language. For that, you need to read the books by Steve and Sally. Instead, I show you some of the ways that I use important features of the object modeling language. I also provide some guidance in how to deal with a few thorny issues.

Experience on multiple projects has taught me many things. One of the most important lessons is that you can't skimp on the information models and get away with it. You must ensure that your application requirements are thoroughly captured, in great detail, in your information models. This takes time and hard work. Whenever my colleagues and I have cut corners we have run afoul of the following consequences: (1) the state models become ridiculously complex; (2) one or two critical requirements lie hidden until late in the modeling process, leading to time-consuming rework; (3) new requirements that should have been anticipated arise late in the modeling process and wreak havoc. On the other hand, a good information model leads to simple, stable state models. This book focuses on building good information models because that is the key to success.

Coming from a function-oriented programming background, learning to build information models has been challenging to say the least. I've noticed that engineers new to the Shlaer-Mellor method grapple with many of the same questions that I did: What model structures are legal? (Can I do *that* with a supertype relationship?) How much detail should go into information model? How do I build a model that won't fall apart when the requirements change? What's the difference between a good information model and a bad information model? Why do I need to write object descriptions? How do I formalize a relationship between exactly three (not zero one or many - but three) things? What's the best way to model a hierarchy of things? Should I ever model a hierarchy? This book contains answers to these questions and many others.

Another big key to success is to use your time effectively. A common mistake is to spend too much time modeling and not enough time doing analysis. Few software engineers appreciate the value of distinguishing the activities of analysis and modeling. I don't know how many times I've seen a novice analyst spend hours building the perfect model to suit a set of *perceived* requirements. Later on the requirements change, or they turn out to be the wrong requirements, or they turn out to be based on some aspect of the system that is so volatile that no attempt to nail down the requirements can be successful. As a consequence the whole model unravels. I wrote Part 2 to show how this kind of disaster can be avoided.

To become a good programmer, not only do you need to write a lot of code, but you also need to look at code written by other people. The same is true when it comes to analysis and modeling. The models in this book will give you something helpful to look at from time to time as you build lots of models. Have fun.

Leon Starr

San Francisco, California

# Acknowledgments

This page is for all of the colleagues and friends that helped me to create this book and get it out the door.

Here is a list of my beta testers (technical reviewers). They were invaluable in the task of rooting out flaws in the text, tables, figures and models: Tonya Bargash, Yeelan Johnson, Michael Lee, Steve Mellor, Walt Murphy, Linda Ruark, Jonathon Sandoe, Sally Shlaer and Phil Zakhour.

Highly entertaining conversations with Michael Lee about project management, politics, training and technical issues provided considerable guidance and inspiration, which fueled my enthusiasm throughout this project.

Thousands of hours of intensely focused project work with most of my reviewers, as well as Ruth Knipe, provided me with the analysis and modeling experience that made this book possible. Tracy Yim deserves credit for convincing me to start this project and for providing support and encouragement all along the way.

I am thoroughly indebted to Walt Murphy for his highly technical and meticulous evaluation of every chapter and for creating the index.

I would like to thank Kollar Design Associates for the front cover design, Karen Cornell for the back cover design, and I would like to thank Judith Jauhal for the author's photograph.

Finally, but most importantly, I want to thank Steve Mellor and Sally Shlaer for all the training, support and especially their method.

# Basic model structures

1

# Objects

**What is an object?**

Consider a set of things, all of which share the same characteristics, behave the same way, and conform to the same rules and policies. Let's go get a bunch of things - cameras for example, and put them together into just such a set:

### A bunch of cameras

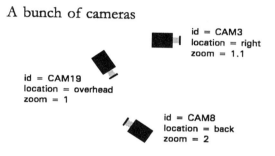

id = CAM3
location = right
zoom = 1.1

id = CAM19
location = overhead
zoom = 1

id = CAM8
location = back
zoom = 2

**Figure 1.1**

Each camera is a distinct real-world entity. Each camera has its own location and zoom setting. By policy, each camera is tagged with a unique label - its ID (identifier).

It's hard not to stare at Figure 1.1 without abstracting a prototypical camera. This abstraction is what the Shlaer-Mellor method calls an *object*. Here's the notation for our prototypical camera:

**The object symbol**

> **Camera**
>
> * ID
> - Location
> - Zoom

This symbol states that there is a thing called a Camera. It also says that every Camera has an ID value, a Location value and a Zoom value. Just as importantly, it asserts that all Cameras behave the same way and conform to the same rules and policies.

**The difference between objects and instances**

It is important not to confuse the prototypical camera - the Camera object - with a specific camera - an *instance* of Camera.

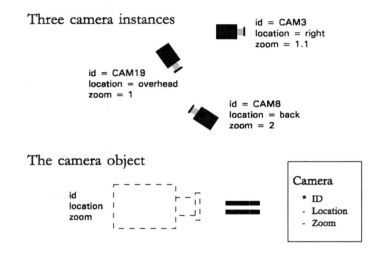

**Figure 1.2**

**Anatomy of an object table**

Tables make it easy to organize data about object instances.

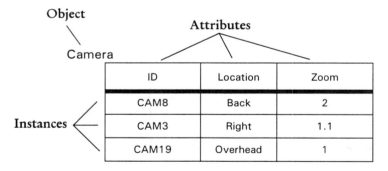

Each row in an object's table contains data about one instance of the object. Each column of the table contains values for each instance corresponding to a single attribute.

# Object table rules

The rules described in this section are borrowed from the relational model of data.[1] These rules keep the formalism uniform and minimal. Uniformity means that we keep one real-world fact in one place. So when we update a piece of information, we won't have to worry about cleaning up any loose ends. Minimalism means that we build models using a handful of simple, rigorously defined constructs. With a little skill, these constructs can be assembled like building blocks to describe extremely complex applications. Finally, if we faithfully follow our table rules, we ensure that our models can be translated into implementation structures - like program language statements - in a straightforward manner. Let's move on to the first rule.

**All attribute values are atomic**

The data found at a row-column intersection has no structure (or at least no structure that has meaning in the domain[2] in which it is modeled). Here's an example object taken from a household inventory application:

Inventory Item

| ID | Location | Condition |
| --- | --- | --- |
| OW8 | Cellar | Excellent |
| CD19S | Lroom | Good |
| SCUS | Closet | Okay |

If you retrieve a value like CD19S from the Item ID column, all you know is that you have found the item CD19S. You can print it, transmit it, store it, retrieve it, and use it as an index into some other table. In all these cases you are dealing with one unit of information.

This rule helps us maintain the integrity of data in our models, and it also simplifies the rules governing data access. Beyond these reasons, which have to do with database theory, the data atomicity rule forces us to model our application more precisely.

---

[1] C.J. Date, *An Introduction to Database Systems*, Addison-Wesley, Reading, MA, 1977.

[2] That's subject matter domain (not attribute domain). A single fact in a client domain may be parsed into multiple facts that make sense in a service domain.

So what do you do if your domain needs to know the internal format of a piece of data? Simple - you model it. Let's say that instead of a household inventory system you are designing a system to organize your audio library.

In that case, you would have to break down Item.ID using a table like this:

Album

| ID | Medium | Compilation Type |
|----|--------|------------------|
| A19 | CD | Single |
| A34 | Record | Multi |
| A55 | Record | Single |

The information encoded as CD19S has been analyzed to extract the relevant attributes. It turns out that all these attributes describe a single object named Album.

Sometimes an encoded format breaks down into attributes corresponding to multiple objects and relationships. A part number in a catalog, for example, might contain attributes pertaining to a Manufacturer, Supplier, and Part.

**Instance order is ignored**

Since an object table represents the contents of an unordered set like this...

**A set of instances**

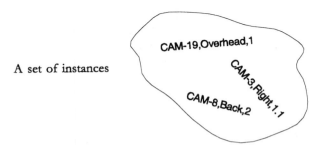

Figure 1.3

...it makes sense that the following tables are equivalent.

| ID | Location | Zoom Setting |
|---|---|---|
| CAM8 | Back | 2 |
| CAM3 | Right | 1.1 |
| CAM19 | Overhead | 1 |

**=**

| ID | Location | Zoom Setting |
|---|---|---|
| CAM19 | Overhead | 1 |
| CAM8 | Back | 2 |
| CAM3 | Right | 1.1 |

**Attribute order is ignored**     The same reasoning applies to attributes.  An object table header constitutes an unordered set of attributes.

**A set of unordered attributes**

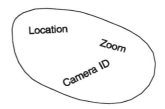

So these two table headings are equivalent:

| ID | Location | Zoom |
|---|---|---|

**=**

| Location | Zoom | ID |
|---|---|---|

**Each instance is unique**     An entity can be represented only once in a table.  This idea is rooted in the relational model of data, which is in turn rooted in set theory.  There can be no duplicate elements in a set.

| ID | Location | Zoom |
|---|---|---|
| CAM8 | Back | 2 |
| CAM8 | Back | 2 |
| CAM19 | Overhead | 1 |

No duplicate instances allowed

To enforce this rule, we define and use identifiers.  For a description of identifiers, see "Identification role" on page 25.

# Object categories

Novice analysts aren't always playing with a full deck.

What I mean is that, in the context of information modeling, they often ignore types of objects that would make complex requirements easy to capture. To become a good analyst, you need to learn when to use - and when not to use - several categories of objects.

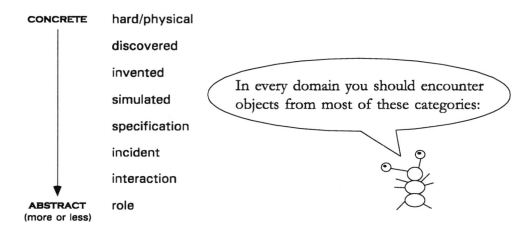

**Figure 1.4**

The categories I am about to describe are not rigorously defined. They are empirically derived from the models I have produced and reviewed over the last 10 years. As a novice, I depended too much on the more concrete categories. With increased experience I found that the abstract categories were necessary to address sophisticated systems.

You may find objects that fit more than one category or are difficult to categorize. Don't worry about it. I don't want you to memorize this list or walk around with it taped to your head. It is important, however, to avoid the novice trap of seeing only the physical objects in a system.

**Hard or physical objects**
A *hard or physical object* is one that you can kick. They tend to come in closely related clusters: Elevator, Floor, Shaft for example... here's another cluster: Mirror, Laser, Motor. Not surprisingly, physical objects appear in any domain that controls or tracks physical things.

An elevator control application would consist of physical objects like Elevator, Floor, Building and Shaft. But physical objects are not restricted to high-level application domains. A low-level robot control service domain might consist of objects like Robot, Arm, and Gripper. This service might be used by an application like Factory Material Transport, which also has physical objects like Part, Subassembly and Process Station. On the other hand, it might be used by an artificial intelligence application with more abstract objects like Goal, Condition and Path.

SOFT OBJECTS

A *soft object* is one that you can't kick. Sometimes they are already defined and sometimes you need to invent them. All the following object categories are soft (nonphysical).

**Discovered objects**

*Discovered objects* are defined by application experts long before the analysts arrive on the scene. An operating system domain needs objects like Process, Semaphore, and Queue. An accounting application needs objects like Account, Asset, Liability, and Corporation. You can't kick any of these things, but in every other sense they are just like physical objects.

Discovered objects generally appear in domains that don't directly track or control the physical world. Some examples are board games, accounting, flight simulators and other types of simulators.

**Invented objects**

Sometimes you invent objects to make a system of rules work. In an animation record and playback service domain, my team invented objects like Parameter, Event, Timeline, and Animatable Entity. The behavior and attributes of these objects were defined according to rules that we invented to fulfill the requirements of this domain. In fact, the application that used the animation service was also full of *invented objects*. This application generated special-effects images for professional video, so we abstracted objects like Camera, Light, Screen and Stage, which behaved according to our invented rules.

Invented objects often appear in service domains. The analysts are free to invent whatever objects are necessary to support the requirements imposed on the service domain.

**Simulated objects**

Say that you are building a flight simulator. You model the object Airplane. Is that a hard object or a soft object? Since you are building a simulator, you would model the Airplane that you were interested in supporting. While it would be inspired by your knowledge of real-

9

world airplanes, you will probably model your own special version. Your airplane might be a simplified version of the real thing or it might do things that a real-world airplane doesn't (like fly under water). It is soft in the sense that it is not intended to be a real-world airplane (as would be the case if you were building an onboard navigation system for real planes). It is discovered in the sense that you didn't invent the airplane concept. It is invented in the sense that you have poetic license with the concept. So we have a new soft category called "simulated".

**Specification objects**  A *specification object* is a design, plan, blueprint, scheme or definition of one or more less abstract objects. Here is a specification of an aircraft:

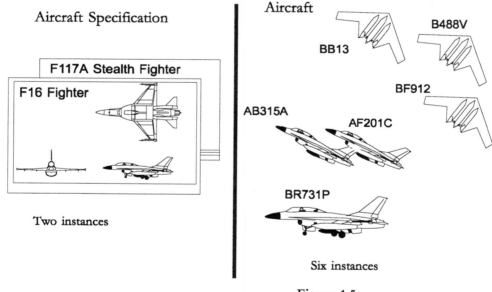

Figure 1.5

The information model looks like this:

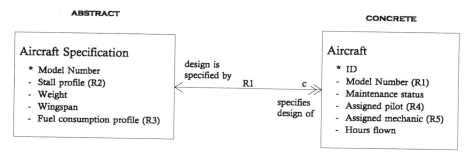

**Model 1.1**

Being a hard object, an instance of Aircraft is something that you can kick. An Aircraft Specification, on the other hand, is nonkickable. An Aircraft Specification is simply a set of blueprints and design parameters.

The specification object and relationship are a generic pattern with the following form:

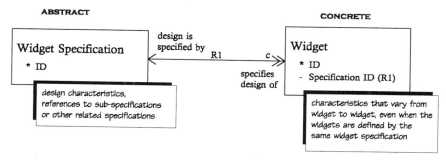

**Model 1.2**

The specification object takes on the name of the tangible object suffixed by something like

Model, Type, Class, Design, Template, Specification

The relationship between Aircraft Specification and Aircraft is a standard form called a *specification relationship*. The specification relationship is almost always 1:Mc. In other words, the tangible thing is defined by exactly one specification, whereas the specification defines zero, one or many things. A blueprint can exist long before it is realized.

On a real project this simple two-object pattern is a nice start, but it usually becomes more interesting. Like physical objects, specification objects tend to clump together.

Say that you are building a flight simulator that gives you tools to design your own plane. You will need an information model that constrains the kinds of planes that can be built. Rather than having a single object called Aircraft Specification, you would need a system of objects and relationships defining how a plane can legally be constructed. You would have a number of specification objects like Wing Type, Fuselage Type, and Aerodynamic Profile that interrelate to form an Aircraft Specification.

On a typical information model you find a cluster of specification objects that define and restrict a legal assembly of several physical, invented, discovered, or simulated objects.

**Widget assembly rules
(specification objects)**

Lots of rules

Assembled widget
(physical objects)

Not so many rules

Types of questions this part
of the model can answer:

How big/small can a widget be?

In what areas can certain features be located?

What are the acceptable tolerances?

What kinds of devices can it interface with?

Types of questions this part
of the model can answer:

How big/small is this widget?

Where are certain features actually located on this widget

What specific device is this widget connected to?

**This is a common object model pattern**

**Figure 1.6**

Specification objects don't have much behavior. Instances of specification objects tend to be written rarely and read frequently. To the degree that editing of specifications is allowed, the editing operations are reflected in the state and process models of the specification objects. It is often the case that specification objects are written only by the system developers prior to runtime.[1] When this is the case, there is probably no need to build the specification object state models. If reading is the only runtime operation on a specification object, then you can put the read actions in the state models of the referencing nonspecification objects.

Important: Novice analysts often ignore specification objects. It's all too easy to construct an object like the following:

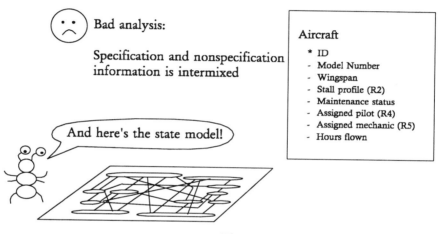

Bad analysis:

Specification and nonspecification information is intermixed

And here's the state model!

Aircraft

* ID
- Model Number
- Wingspan
- Stall profile (R2)
- Maintenance status
- Assigned pilot (R4)
- Assigned mechanic (R5)
- Hours flown

Figure 1.7

The identification of specification object clusters is critical. If you embed specification information and relationships in your tangible objects, you will end up with complex and weird relationships. The state models will be ugly. Trust me.

Specification objects are found in all domains.

**Incident objects**  An incident is something that happens. Should a dynamic thing like an incident appear in an information model? If an incident is truly transitory, it is best modeled as an event in a state model. We model an event as an object only when it brings with it attributes and relationships important to our application. Here are some examples:

---

[1]You can shorten your schedule by omitting edit functions (and hence the supporting state models) to users in early system releases. In this case, the developers instantiate read-only data by hand or through the use of quick and dirty utilities.

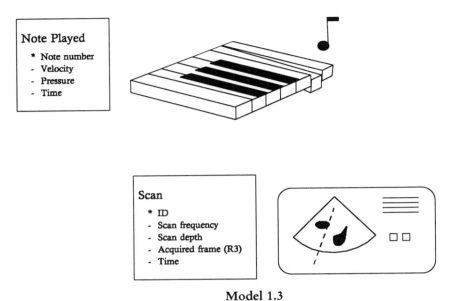

**Note Played**

* Note number
- Velocity
- Pressure
- Time

**Scan**

* ID
- Scan frequency
- Scan depth
- Acquired frame (R3)
- Time

**Model 1.3**

In each of these cases, time is an attribute. Compared to physical and specification objects, incident objects are rare.

If you find that many of the objects in a domain have time as an attribute, then you probably need an archival service domain. The archival service will record Events concerning activities in a client domain. As a result, you don't have to model time in the client.

**Interaction objects**  An interaction object is a consequence of a relationship.  Consider this example:

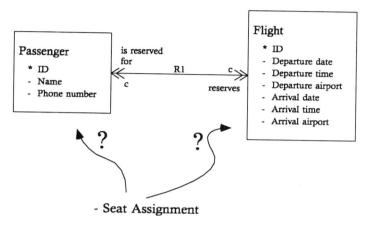

**Model 1.4**

Where do we put an attribute like seat assignment?  We can't associate it with customer, because a customer may make more than one reservation.  We can't associate it with flight, because there are many seat assignment possibilities on a flight.  We have the same problem with an attribute like cost and payment status.  In fact, these attributes are not attributes of either object; rather they are attributes of the reservation relationship itself. How do we assign attributes to a relationship? We create an object to represent the interaction:

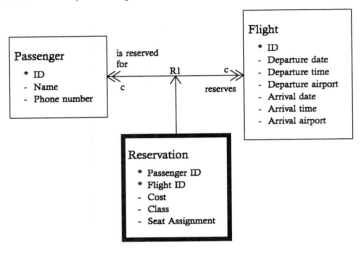

**Model 1.5**

Here are some more examples:

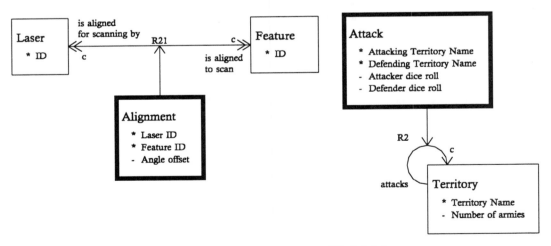

**Model 1.6**

Interactions are always modeled using associative objects. They occur to a small degree in most domains.

**Role objects**  Sometimes an object has more than one personality. It is difficult to model such a schizophrenic object as a single entity because the unifying behavior varies so much depending on the time or other circumstances.

**Scenario 1: Changing Relevance** An object takes on relationships or descriptive attributes during one period of time, and during another period of time these same relationships or attributes are irrelevant.

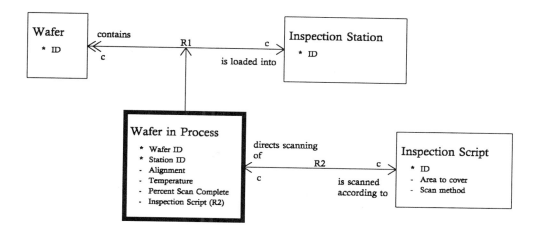

**Model 1.7**

When the Wafer is loaded, it has a relationship to an Inspection Station, so an instance of Wafer in Process is created. The attributes Alignment, Temperature and Percent Scan Complete are assigned values and kept up to date. When the Wafer is removed from the Inspection Station, relationship R2 and the Wafer in Process attributes are no longer relevant. But that's okay because we delete the instance of Wafer in Process, leaving behind only the Wafer instance. It's better to vaporize irrelevant attributes in this manner than to leave them lying around with useless values that the state and process models have to remember to ignore! That's what would happen if we tried to do without the Wafer in Process object.

**Scenario 2: Different Personality** Common behavior can be defined for all instances of an object, but there is also special behavior that applies to subsets of instances. The defining behavior of an instance never varies over time.

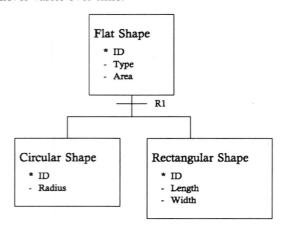

**Model 1.8**

In this case the instances have *nonmigrating* roles. Once an instance of Circular Shape is created, it never changes into any other type of Flat Shape.

**Scenario 3: Relative Roles** An instance of one object is composed of or otherwise relates to strict numeric arrangements of some other object.

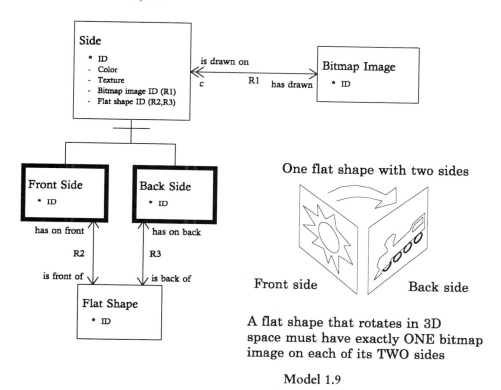

A flat shape that rotates in 3D space must have exactly ONE bitmap image on each of its TWO sides

Model 1.9

In this example, all Sides behave the same way. But it is important that every Front Side be paired with a Back Side on a Screen. To see why object roles are the only precise way to model this situation, see Chapter 13 on page 209.

Roles are usually modeled using super/subtype relationships, but sometimes are modeled using an associative object.

Failure to recognize role objects often results in imprecise information models and excessively complex state models.

## Frequently asked questions about objects

**Is it okay to have an object with only one attribute?**

Yes. There are actually two questions to consider. First, is it legal to construct a single-attribute object? Second, assuming that it is legal, is it useful? Let's consider the following object from a board game like Monopoly.[1]

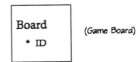

(Game Board)

A single attribute object is legal because it doesn't break any of our table rules. We can construct a table with a single column.

| Board ID |
|----------|
| 8 |
| 2 |
| 3 |

The table is legal. What about the object? An object is a bunch of things with the same behavior and the same characteristics. We can argue that a Game Board fits this criterion.

The more relevant question is whether a single-attribute object has any utility. In the game example, we are concerned with things that happen on the game board. We have objects like Space, Player, Token, Hotel, House, and Property. The Board doesn't seem relevant because we are concerned only with the contents of the board. We care about how all the elements of a board and the game interact. We need to know the Space where a Token is located or the Player that owns a House. We move a Token, we track allocation of Property, but what do we do with a Board?

Furthermore, while we have multiple instances of the other objects, we notice that there is only ever one instance of Board. This is because we are thinking only of one game being played at a time which suits the immediate requirements.

So it seems that we can do without the Board object. But what happens when our requirements extend so that we must accommodate multiple games in progress? On a network perhaps? Then we need the Board object to distinguish the status of the same instance of Token in two active games.

---

[1]Monopoly™ is a registered trademark of Parker Brothers.

Another possibility is that Board has some attributes that aren't apparent at first. Money placed in the center of the board might be available to players under certain conditions, like when someone stops at Free Parking. In this case an amount of cash would be an attribute of Board. Even if there are no descriptive attributes, there may be referential attributes. If you wanted to model a rule that at all times there is exactly one player that can move or conduct transactions, you could do it with a relationship like this...

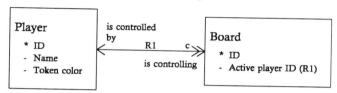

**Model 1.10**

When you model an application, the objects at the focus of your concern tend to have lots of obvious attributes and relationships. There are always a few on the horizon that don't seem to add much value at first. They should be included in your model because more than likely they will prove useful homes for attributes and relationships that, while not central to the area of study, are nonetheless critical. Of course, if it turns out that a single-attribute object like Board never serves any purpose, then you can always discard it when you complete the model.

**Can an object have only one instance?**

Yes. Again, there is no problem as far as the formalism goes. An empty table or a table that always contains only one instance is perfectly fine. If there is always one instance, you have to ask why. Many times it is because the functions at the focus of your interest only apply to one instance. But, as you extend your scope, it becomes apparent that more than one instance is possible.

If we are building a control system for an inspection station, we may know there is only ever one station. But the minute we extend this system to networked control of many stations, more instances are entered into the table.

It is also possible that you have a useless object that really shouldn't be an object. The following object is a bad idea:

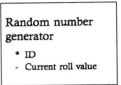

Instead we really have an attribute of something else:

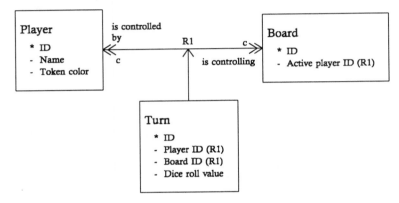

**What does it mean when an object is drawn with a dashed border?**

When you split an information model into multiple subsystems, you will need off-page objects. An off-page object is like an off-page connector in any symbol language. Off-page objects are drawn with dashed lines.

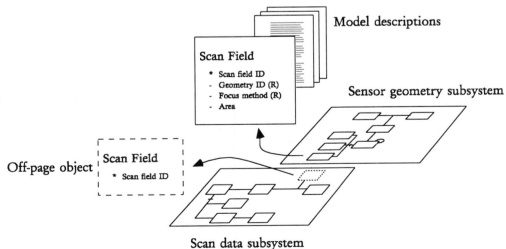

# Chapter 2                                               Attributes

**What is an attribute?**      Let's start with a dictionary[1] definition...

> **at·trib·ute** n. 1. A quality or characteristic inherent in or ascribed to someone or something.

For our purposes, we substitute "someone or something" with the phrase "all of the instances of a single object". It is easier to define with a picture:

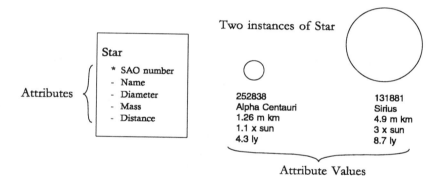

**Figure 2.1**

It is important to distinguish between an attribute and a value assigned to an attribute. An *attribute* is a prototypical characteristic relevant to all possible instances of an object. An *attribute value* is a characteristic of a specific instance in the set.

Attributes have the following properties:

- purpose

- identification role

- dependency on other attributes

- value assignment

---

[1] The American Heritage® Dictionary of the English Language, Third Edition (electronic version 4.0), Houghton Mifflin Company, Boston, 1992.

- universal meaning
- origin

Let's explore them.

# Purpose

An attribute either names or describes object instances.

**Descriptive attributes**

An attribute may tell us about the nature of an object, like its physical appearance, operational status, geometric characteristics, and temporal situation. Here are some examples:

> Size, Wait Time, X Coordinate, Color, Angle Offset, Street Address, Stall Speed

We call these *descriptive attributes*.

**Naming attributes**

An attribute may attempt to distinguish one instance of an object from another. Here are some examples:

> Company Name, File Name, Driver's License Number, Serial Number, Product Code, Device ID

These attributes exist not so much to describe, but to identify, instances. We call these *naming attributes*. A naming attribute may or may not be sufficient to uniquely identify instances of an object. For example, the attribute Employee Name is a naming attribute, but it is possible to have two employees with the same name.

Naming attributes are usually suffixed with a word like ID, name, code or number.

Some naming attributes exist prior to analysis:

> Company Name, Floor Number, Driver's License Number, Aircraft ID

These are *discovered names* because they are discovered by the analyst.

Other naming attributes are invented by the analyst to ensure that each object has at least one identifier. Some examples are

> Camera ID, Event ID, Transaction ID, Segment ID

These are *invented names*. By convention, I stick with the suffix *ID* for all invented names (rather than number, code, etc.) just to keep my models consistent.

**Naming or descriptive?** The purpose of an attribute is not always clear. At first glance, the following attribute appears to be a naming attribute:

Runway Number

Consider three runways at an airport, 27, 90 and 19. Each of these numbers seems to be an arbitrary name. But airport runways are numbered by compass direction. Runway 27 is oriented to the west at 270 degrees.

If I cared enough about it, I would argue that Runway Number is really a descriptive attribute since it describes a geometric characteristic of a runway. Whether it's a naming or descriptive attribute doesn't really matter. What's important is that the attribute in this example does more than just provide a name.

# Identification role

As stated in Chapter 1, every instance of an object is unique. If we have three instances of the Camera object, we know that each instance represents a distinct physical Camera. This concept of distinctness is an important aspect of the real world that we would like to capture in our analysis models. Identifiers make it possible to formalize uniqueness in the table formalism.

An *identifier* is a set of one or more attributes guaranteed to select exactly one instance of an object. Identifiers make it possible to formalize relationships between objects.

Using table examples, we will explore both *single-attribute identifiers* and *compound (multiple-attribute) identifiers*.

**Single attribute identifiers**

The Camera object introduced in the last section has a single-attribute identifier, Camera ID, which is shown with some example instances in the table below.

| Camera | | ID | Location | Zoom |
|---|---|---|---|---|

**Camera**
  * ID
  - Location
  - Zoom

| ID | Location | Zoom |
|---|---|---|
| CAM8 | Back | 2 |
| CAM3 | Right | 1.1 |
| CAM19 | Overhead | 1 |

**Model 2.1**

Any value selected for Camera.ID, CAM8 let's say, leads us to a single instance of Camera. Consequently, you can never have more than one CAM8 in the Camera.ID column.

Zoom is not an identifier because it is possible to have two cameras with the same Zoom value. The same goes for Location.

**Compound identifiers**

A compound identifier consists of two or more attributes. A value must be supplied for each of these component attributes to guarantee that a unique instance is selected.

The Folder object has a compound identifier that consists of two attributes: Folder.ID and Drawer ID.

**Folder**
  * ID
  - Drawer ID (R1)
  - Name

| ID | Drawer ID | Name |
|---|---|---|
| F2 | D1 | food to go |
| F2 | D2 | food delivered |
| F1 | D1 | parking tickets |

**Model 2.2**

It takes both a Folder.ID and a Drawer ID to guarantee the selection of a unique instance in the Folder table.

**Multiple identifiers**     An object can have more than one identifier as shown below:

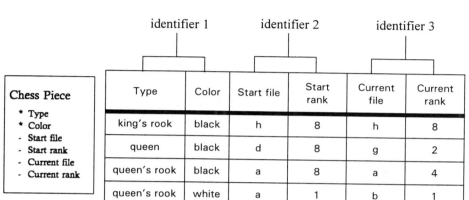

Model 2.3

In this table of chess pieces you can select a unique piece by specifying the piece type and color, or the start file and rank (no two pieces can start on the same rank and file) or the current file and rank piece position.

When an object has more than one identifier, only one - the *primary identifier* - is indicated on the information model diagram. The primary identifier formalizes most (usually all) relationships. All identifiers, primary and otherwise, should be listed in the beginning of the object description. While only one identifier is necessary for relationship formalization purposes, it is important to document *all* identifiers to ensure that attribute dependency properties are properly formed. Attribute dependency is defined a little later in this chapter.

**Overlapping identifiers**     An attribute may participate in zero, one or many identifiers. In the "many" case, we get an overlap as demonstrated below.

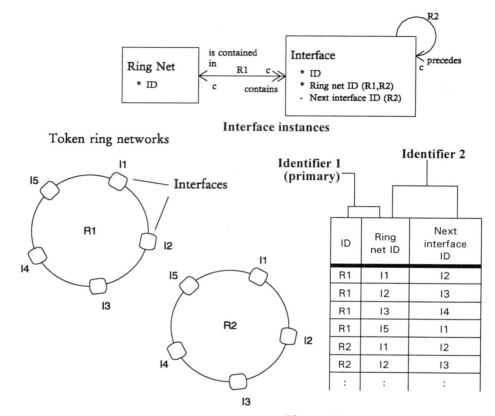

Figure 2.2

The Interface.Ring Net ID takes part in each of the two compound identifiers in the table. The Interface.ID cannot be a single-attribute identifier all by itself because the interfaces are renumbered (1, 2, 3...) for each token ring network. To get a unique interface out of this table, you need the Interface.Ring Net ID and either the Interface.ID or the Interface.Next Interface ID.

For more on modeling networks, see Chapter 15 on page 223.

# Dependence on other attributes

The following normalization rules ensure that tables are not filled with redundant, inconsistent or missing data. These rules are applied on each object as it is abstracted.

**Dependence on the identifier**

All nonidentifying attributes depend on the identifier (and nothing but the identifier).

| | **Light** |
|---|---|
| * | ID |
| - | Color temperature |
| - | Intensity |
| - | x |
| - | y |
| - | z |

| ID | Color temperature | Intensity | x | y | z |
|----|-------------------|-----------|---|---|---|
| L4 | 1400 | 3 | 13 | 25 | 1 |
| L1 | 800 | 7 | 55 | 3 | 1.7 |

**Figure 2.3**

All the nonidentifying attributes in the Light object (Color Temperature, Intensity, x, y, and z) are dependent on the value selected for Light.ID and nothing else. The value of Intensity is not affected by the X coordinate, for example. Picture the dependencies like this:

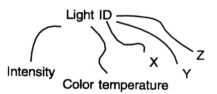

Note that there are no interdependencies among the nonidentifying attributes.

29

The following object does not fit this rule:

Contact

\* ID
- Name
- Home phone
- Birthdate
- Company
- Work address

| ID | Name | Home phone | Birthdate | Company | Work address |
|----|------|-----------|-----------|---------|--------------|
| C33 | Bob Irving | 216-2212 | 3/18/63 | LaST Computers | 345 Silicon Sludge Lane |
| C14 | Judith Jauhal | 216-9902 | 12/23/65 | DivideByZero Software | 10323 Faultline Road |
| C19 | Mike Libby | 302-8890 | 2/16/51 | LaST Computers | 345 Silicon Sludge Lane |

**Figure 2.4**

In this case there is a dependency between Company and Work Address.

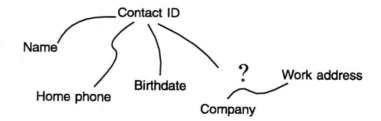

This is bad for a couple of reasons. First, the work address data are redundantly specified whenever I add multiple contacts that work at the same company. If LaST computers moves to a new location, an unknown number of address fields must be updated. Second, if I delete the last person that works at DivideByZero Computers from my database, I unnecessarily lose the address information for that company.

When attributes cling together within an object, you have to abstract a new object:

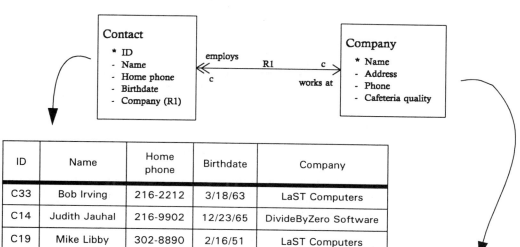

| ID | Name | Home phone | Birthdate | Company |
|----|------|-----------|-----------|---------|
| C33 | Bob Irving | 216-2212 | 3/18/63 | LaST Computers |
| C14 | Judith Jauhal | 216-9902 | 12/23/65 | DivideByZero Software |
| C19 | Mike Libby | 302-8890 | 2/16/51 | LaST Computers |

| Name | Work address | Phone | Cafeteria quality |
|------|-------------|-------|-------------------|
| LaST Computers | 345 Silicon Sludge Lane | 202-9999 | Yechh! |
| DivideByZero Software | 10323 Faultline Road | 430-8818 | Okay |

**Figure 2.5**

Now there are no redundant data. This also sets me up to discover useful attributes that describe a Company that are much farther removed from the Contact (Cafeteria Quality, for example). As illustrated below, the nonidentifying attributes depend only on the identifier in each table.

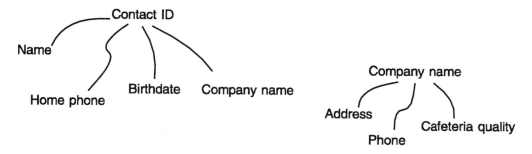

**Dependence on the whole identifier**   Each nonidentifying attribute must depend on the whole ID. This rule is violated in the object below.

| Automated Vehicle on Route |
|---|
| \* Vehicle ID |
| \* Route ID |
| - Speed |
| - Distance |
| - Battery charge |

| Vehicle ID | Route ID | Speed | Distance | Battery charge |
|---|---|---|---|---|
| V15 | R503 | 10.23 | 45.2 | 80% |
| V52 | R34 | 15.07 | 721.8 | 12% |

**Figure 2.6**

Battery Charge has nothing to do with a Route. Battery Charge is really a property of Vehicle. Speed and Distance (along Route) are dependent on both the Vehicle ID and Route ID.

Partial dependence

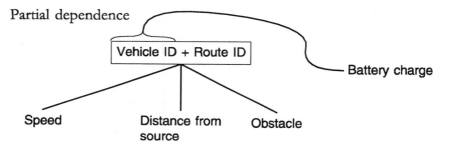

The Battery Charge attribute really belongs in the Vehicle object. Otherwise, we would unnecessarily lose the Battery Charge information when a Vehicle was taken off a Route.

Here are the correct objects:

| Automated Vehicle on Route | | Vehicle ID | Route ID | Speed | Distance |
|---|---|---|---|---|---|
| | | V15 | R503 | 10.23 | 45.2 |
| | | V52 | R34 | 15.07 | 721.8 |

**Automated Vehicle on Route**

* \* Vehicle ID
* \* Route ID
* - Speed
* - Distance

| ID | Weight | Load | Battery charge |
|---|---|---|---|
| V15 | 2.4 | empty | 80% |
| V52 | 3.7 | L155 | 12% |

**Vehicle**
* \* ID
* - Weight
* - Load (R2)
* - Battery charge

# Value assignment

What are the consequences when you assign a value to an attribute? It depends on whether that attribute is part of an identifier. Let's take a look at each case.

**Changing a nonidentifier value**

Consider changing the value of a nonidentifier attribute like Zoom in the Camera object. Let's take the instance CAM8 and change its Zoom from 2 to 1.

**Camera**
* \* ID
* - Location
* - Zoom

| ID | Location | Zoom |
|---|---|---|
| CAM8 | Back | 2 →1 |
| CAM3 | Right | 1.1 |
| CAM19 | Overhead | 1 |

No big deal. You should be able to change the value of a nonidentifier attribute without affecting any other attribute values in the same object.[1] Some exceptions are made to this rule when it comes to computational dependency.

---

[1] Coordination with attributes in other objects may, however, be triggered through the Camera's state machine actions.

**Changing an identifier value**

But it is a big deal when you change the value of an identifier attribute. Let's take the same instance and change the Camera.ID attribute. Can we change CAM8 to CAM3? No! That would cause us to have two Camera 3's, which is an impossibility (according to our table rules). Since there can be only one Camera 3, the end result may be that we have to delete one of the two instances. Not good.

Okay, well what if we change CAM8 to CAM6? This isn't so bad because CAM6 didn't previously exist. But notice that by changing the value of the identifier we have, in effect, deleted one instance (CAM8) and created a new instance (CAM6).

So keep this in mind...

Mess with the identifier and you mess with the whole instance.

What about changing only part of an identifier?

**Vehicle License**

* State
* Number
- Date issued

It's the same thing. If we take an instance of Vehicle License and change the value of its State attribute, we are, in effect, creating a new instance of Vehicle License. The same goes for the Number attribute. This makes sense since all non-ID attributes depend on the whole identifier.

The ant's rule applies and leads to the following consequence:

> In the state and process models the manipulation of identifier values is performed exclusively by create and delete actions.

# Universal meaning

Does every attribute of an object instance require a meaningful value at all times? I would like to just say "yes", but the real answer to that question is "Yes, uhm... pretty much..." The principle of universally meaningful attributes varies in severity as we explore different kinds of attributes.

**Always applicable**

An attribute that is always applicable will always hold a meaningful value no matter how the object is behaving or what relationships the object holds. Here is an example:

Landing Gear.Mode (Extending, Retracting, Up, Down)

Landing Gear.Movement Status (Jammed, Not Jammed)

If we presume that the object refers to landing gear in a fully assembled and operational aircraft, as opposed to being a part sitting on a conveyor belt, we can always assign a meaningful value to each attribute. An object made up of attributes that are always applicable is probably well defined.

While we would like for all attributes to have this property, sometimes trade-offs have to be made. In these cases you need to consider less ideal attribute possibilities.

**Never applicable (for some instances)**

Sometimes you abstract an object where the instances all behave the same way and have all the same characteristics - except for one attribute that doesn't apply in some cases.

Consider this object taken from a submarine game:

```
Torpedo
  * ID
  - Guide wire remaining
  - Fuel remaining
```

As we write the object description, we find that one of the attributes is meaningless for some instances:

A torpedo is designed to operate in one of two ways. One type of torpedo is unguided. It uses its own sensors to find a target. The other type is guided by a wire that is reeled out the rear of the torpedo as it swims. At some point the wire runs out, is cut, and then the torpedo follows a preprogrammed search pattern until it runs out of fuel or hits a target.

The Guide Wire Remaining attribute does not apply to the first type of torpedoes (self-guided).

To fix the problem you could assign the value N/A (not applicable) to the Guide Wire Remaining attribute for all self-guided torpedoes. Or perhaps you could permanently assign 0 to such instances. Neither approach is advisable, however.

Whenever you discover an attribute that requires the assignment of N/A or a constant with special meaning (-1, 0, 1, 999999, etc.) you have an insufficiently abstracted object. The troublesome attribute points out that not all instances behave the same way.

We can eliminate the troublesome attribute by abstracting objects that reflect the divergent torpedo behavior (as well as the shared behavior).

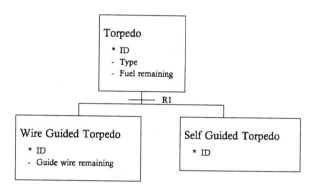

**Model 2.4**

In this case the problem is solved using super/subtyping. Sometimes an associative relationship is more appropriate (see Model 5.3 on page 80).

**Not applicable - at the moment**

An attribute may be applicable for all instances, but not at all times. This is generally due to a change in state. There are certain states where the attribute has no meaning at all.

Let's extend the definition to the landing gear object to include states where the landing gear is not installed in an aircraft...

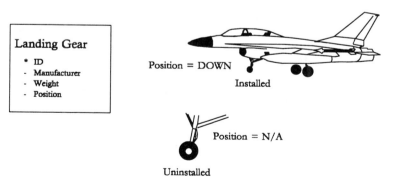

**Model 2.5**

The attribute Position refers to the in-use status of the landing gear (up, down, retracting, extending). This attribute does not apply, however, when we talk about landing gear that has been removed from an aircraft for inspection. Since the gear is detached from the device that moves it into position, the position has no meaning.

We can resolve the problem by assigning an arbitrary value to Position and ignoring it when the landing gear is detached. Or we could create a special position called uninstalled. But these fixes are temporary at best.

Our best bet is to subtype landing gear appropriately:

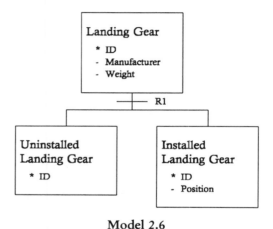

**Model 2.6**

**Delayed assignment**   Sometimes an attribute has meaning, but there is an initial period of time, beyond the creation process, when a value is not yet assigned.

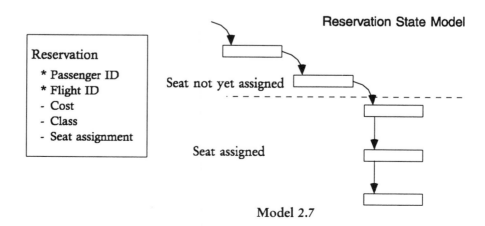

**Model 2.7**

When a flight reservation is made, a seat may or may not be assigned. We could define the attribute domain of Seat Assignment to be: Any aircraft seat name such as 1A, 12C, and so on, or Unassigned.

We can make the attribute more uniform, as in the landing gear example, by subtyping. In this case we could create new objects like Reservation With Seats versus Reservation Without Seats. But is the goal of making a single attribute uniform worth the cost of two more objects and a subtype relationship?

In this case, probably not. But I can never say for sure until I see more of the subsystem and get a feel for what kind of state and process behavior we are going to be modeling. You want the combination of your information model AND state and process models to be simple, yet extensible. If you stick with the Seat Assignment attribute, then you can count on adding a special condition, and maybe even a state or two, to your Reservation state model. But this is probably less effort than subtyping by Seat Assignment.

**More than one meaning**   Sometimes you have an attribute that changes its meaning depending on what value is assigned.

**APPLICATION NOTE**

> At a part inspection station we mark parts that fail inspection. There are two ways to mark a part. You can scratch the part or you can spray ink on the part. If you spray ink, you have a choice of colors. For a given type of part and production process, a script specifies a series of inspection and evaluation steps and a marking scheme.

Here's the initial model:

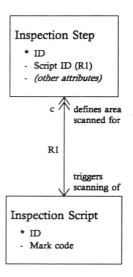

**Model 2.8**

The Inspection Script.Mark Code attribute specifies how a part is to be marked if it fails this script. The attribute domain is 0, 1, 2, 3, 4, 5, where 1 to 3 specifies ink colors, 4 means scratch and 0 means don't mark at all.

Mark Code has a different meaning depending on the kind of marking that is to be applied. So what's wrong with that?

- Model 2.8 doesn't expose all marking possibilities. Can a part be marked more than once? Can a part be both scratched and inked? By burying a scheme in the attribute domain, you hide the rule that a part can be either inked or scratched, but not both.

- The model doesn't extend well. What happens when you get a requirement to mark more than once? Mark and scratch?

- Since marking rules are in the attribute domain, new marking requirements will complicate the attribute domain. This will lead to added complexity in the state model that controls marking.

To make the meaning uniform we could do this:

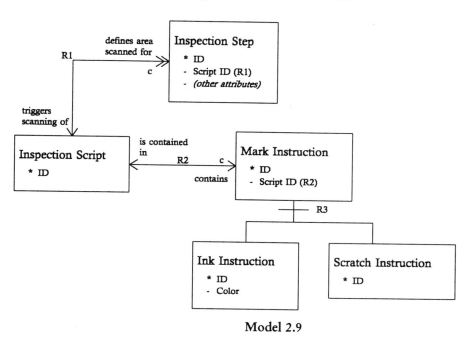

**Model 2.9**

This model takes the application rules that were previously embedded in the Mark Code attribute domain, and exposes them in the objects and relationships.

- 0 - handled by conditional on R2

- 1, 2, 3 - handled by creating instance of Ink Instruction and setting Ink Instruction.Color (note that more colors can easily be added)

- 4 - handled by creating instance of Scratch Instruction (if you had degrees of scratching, heavy/light for example, you could easily add the Scratch Instruction.Degree attribute)

This model easily extends to accommodate new requirements. If we get a requirement to mark more than once, for example, we could change R2 to 1:Mc.

Now I am not saying that the subtype example is necessarily the best approach. But it is important to recognize an attribute with multiple meanings and to be able to expose these meanings using objects and relationships. When I go to this trouble, nine times out of ten I end up discovering hidden application rules. If, by the time you get to the state models, the added objects and relationships don't seem to be adding any value, it's easy to drop them. It's not going to kill you to have one or two multiple-meaning attributes with complex attribute domains lurking in the depths of your information model. But it will kill you if you have lots of this type of attribute. Your information model won't expose subtle, yet important, application rules like it should and it will be difficult to extend as the subsystem assimilates more and more requirements. If you do have a few multiple meaning attributes, keep an eye on them as the requirements develop. Be ready to convert them into more uniform attributes when the model gets weird.

## Origin

The attributes in an object originate in one of two places. If an attribute is both defined and contained in an object, then it is a *native attribute*. If an attribute is defined in some object other than the one in which it is contained, then it is a *referential attribute*.

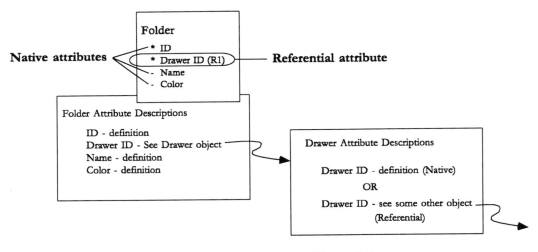

**Figure 2.7**

Native attributes     A native attribute should have a full attribute and domain description. A native attribute can be naming or descriptive. It *may* constitute part or all of an identifier.

Referential attributes     A referential attribute (attribute A) has an attribute description that points to an attribute (attribute B) in the object that the attribute references. Note that attribute B may be either native or referential. If attribute B is referential, then it must point to an attribute (attribute C) in some object. This chain of references can extend through any number of referential attributes, but must eventually resolve to a native attribute somewhere.

A referential attribute can be naming or descriptive It *may* constitute part or all of an identifier.

**Origin and identifiers**

An invented identifier like Point.ID is a native, naming, nonreferential attribute. But other combinations of attribute origin and purpose can yield perfectly good identifiers:

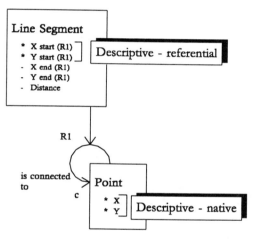

**Model 2.10**

In this example, the identifier of the Point object is made up of descriptive native attributes. The identifier of the Line Segment object is made up of descriptive referential attributes.

# Summary of Attribute Properties

Take all the attributes in a single object. All of them are eligible as partial or whole identifiers, assuming that they can collectively or individually do what an identifier is supposed to do. Some of these attributes are referenced and some are native. Some are descriptive and some are naming.

You should be able to fill out this form for every attribute in any object:

- Attribute name
- Object it belongs to
- Referential: Y/N
- Part or all of at least one ID for this object: Y/N
- Type Naming/Descriptive
- Description (depends on type); for more details, see Chapter 11

An attribute can have only one of the following identification roles:

- Single-attribute identifier
- Part of one compound identifier
- Part of more than one compound identifier
- Not part of any identifier

An attribute cannot be both a single-attribute identifier AND part of a compound identifier. If an attribute is a single-attribute identifier all by itself, it by definition, needs no other components.

# Frequently asked questions about attributes

**How many attributes can an object have?**

As many as necessary. In my experience this is between 1 and 15, with an average of 5. If I saw an object with 100 attributes, I would expect to find interdependencies among them that would violate the "dependence on identifier and nothing but identifier" rule explained earlier. Nonetheless, if you can pull it off, then the object is legal.

You have to make sure that the object definition holds together. In practice, it breaks down when you have too many attributes.

**How do I know I have all the attributes?**

When there aren't anymore to find. Sorry, no easy answer. This is where you depend on your skill as an analyst - not a modeler. A novice analyst frequently misses important details. An experienced analyst takes good notes, asks good questions, interrogates experts, reads manuals, looks at hardware, and holds productive walkthroughs. For more about this topic, see Chapter 8 on page 143. All these activities are required to get completion. If you just sit there and think them up, scribble them down in an object rectangle, and move on - then you are doomed to miss a lot.

The S-M method seems to
require a lot of invented
ID's. Isn't that inefficient?

No. Here is an example from a system that inspects defects in propellor blades. In this example a defect is a crack or dent.

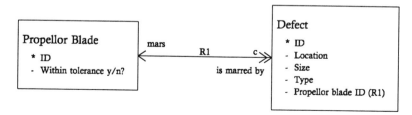

**Model 2.11**

The attribute Defect.ID is invented so that we can distinguish one
defect from another on a propellor blade. We are modeling the real
world. Are defects distinct in the real world? Yes. Therefore, our
model must reflect that fact. How do we do it? We invent an identifier, but only for the purpose of modeling a real-world fact. One real-
world fact - one model construct, you can't get more efficient than
that in the analysis.

But what about the design? If we had to translate every invented identifier into an integer variable, then you would get an inefficient
design. But that is a stupid translation approach and I know you
wouldn't do that. Identifiers can be translated to any number of clever
program-level devices,[1] such as

> array index, memory location, memory offset, pointer, key,
> handle

Okay, but what if my system doesn't ever need to distinguish one
defect from another? Maybe the system measures the degree to which
each propellor is flawed. In that case, don't abstract the Defect object.
Just add an attribute to Propellor.

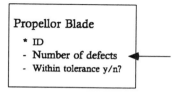

---

[1]Many of which are described in Recursive Design (course notes), Project Technology, Inc., 1994.

*Chapter 3*　　　　　　　　# Relationships

**What is a relationship?**　　It is difficult to define the term relationship. Even the dictionary definition is somewhat circular:

> **re·la·tion·ship** *n.* 1. The condition or fact of being related; connection or association.

The Shlaer-Mellor definition[1] is more specific:

> A *relationship* is the abstraction of an association that holds systematically between instances of objects.

This definition is best understood using an application example:

**APPLICATION NOTE**

A movie player is a system resource that can activate and run a movie. Movies take time to load and, once loaded, take up a lot of memory. But we need the ability to preload up to three movies so that any one of them can be activated from the control room at a moments notice. Only one movie can be run by a movie player at a time.

---

[1]Object Oriented Analysis: Domains and Objects (course notes), Project Technology, Inc., 1995

Here is a sketch of some example application entities that "associate" with one another:

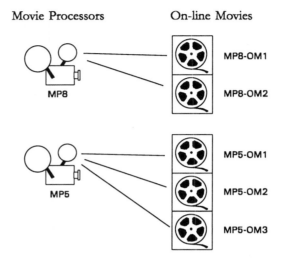

Figure 3.1

This picture suggests a few abstractions. Two movie processors have been drawn, which leads us to abstract the prototypical Movie Processor as an object. Five movies have been drawn, which might lead us to abstract the Movie object - but that's not useful enough. The application note leads us to define the concept of an On-line Movie - a movie that has been loaded into memory and is ready to be played. That gives us the On-line Movie object. (For the purposes of this exercise we don't have to worry about off-line movies, which aren't ready to play).

**Abstracting a relationship**

Figure 3.1 suggests another important abstraction. There are five associations, depicted as straight connecting lines, between the Movie Processors and the On-line Movies. From the perspective of an On-line Movie, each of these lines indicates that the On-line Movie is accessible for immediate playback on the connected Movie Processor. From the perspective of a Movie Processor, each line indicates that the Movie Processor can immediately play the connected On-line Movie. With five of these associations drawn, we can abstract the *prototypical* association and call it a relationship.

**The relationship symbol**   The object and relationship abstractions are illustrated below:

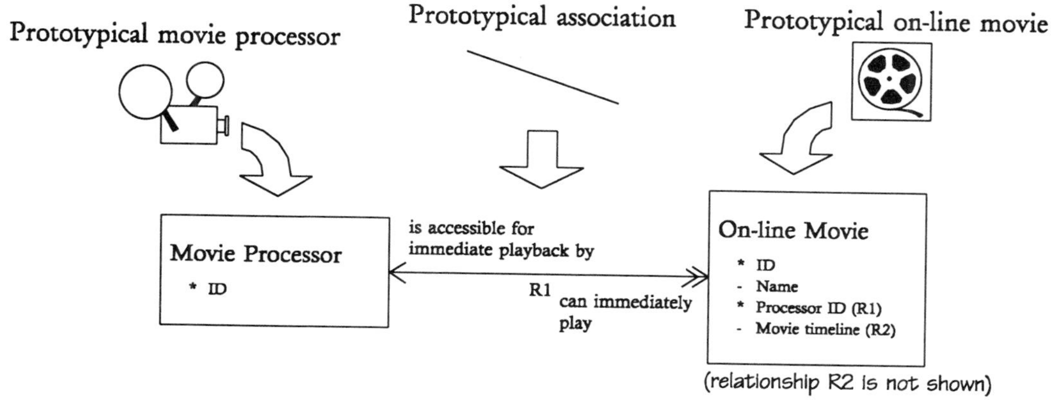

Figure 3.2

**Relationships and rules**   A relationship formalizes real-world rules. Here are the rules formalized by the CAN IMMEDIATELY PLAY relationship in Figure 3.2:

- Every On-line Movie can immediately be played by a Movie Processor.

- An On-line Movie cannot be immediately played by more than one Movie Processor.

- A Movie Processor must have at least one On-line Movie available for immediate execution at all times.

- A Movie Processor may have more than one On-line Movie available for execution.

These rules are defined both graphically - in the way that the relationship arrow is drawn and labeled - and through the placement and definition of the Processor ID attribute in the On-line Movie object. If you are new to Shlaer-Mellor symbology, don't worry about how this all works right now. Subsequent chapters will explain how the different types of relationships are drawn and formalized in nauseating detail.

Here's what's important: A relationship is an abstraction of a real-world association in the same sense that an object is an abstraction of a real-world entity. The process of object abstraction formalizes the characteristics and behavior of real-world entities. The process of relationship abstraction formalizes how these same entities may associate with one another.

# Relationships define application policies

In a typical object-oriented system, people focus so heavily on the objects, that they tend to miss what's happening in the relationships. This is too bad, because the capabilities of a system are largely defined by the number and types of relationships that must be maintained.

I can demonstrate this point by building two different models for part of the same application. Each model will consist of the same basic set of objects. But the relationships in each model will differ, yielding radically different system behavior.

**APPLICATION NOTE**

Presentation graphics application: Predefined shapes can be dragged from a library and positioned on a sheet. Once a shape is placed on the sheet it may be rotated, resized, or moved around.

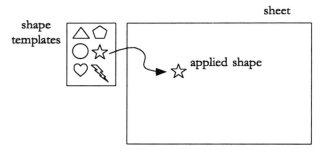

**Figure 3.3**

**Example 1: Master shapes**

In this first example shapes are created from a master shape template. A shape is an ordered set of connected points. The point locations are defined in a local shape coordinate system. Here is how a shape is placed on a sheet:

1. A shape template is selected.

2. An (x,y) location on the sheet is specified for the shape's center.

3. Translate, scale and rotation operations are applied to produce a shape on the sheet.

It might look like this:

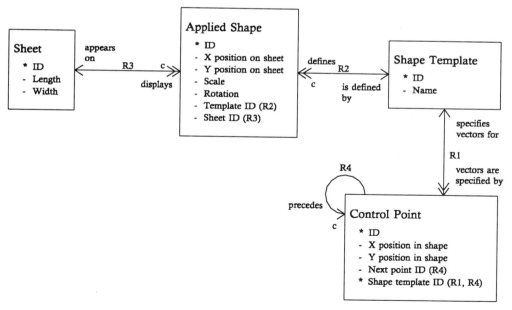

Figure 3.4

Now let's take a look at the information model:

Model 3.1

Each applied shape can be translated, rotated and scaled independently. But a *single* set of control points defines the vertices of multiple applied shapes. Consequently, you can't edit the vertices of any individual applied shape. An edit to the control points in shape template S1 will simultaneously affect applied shapes AS1, AS2 and AS3.

**Example 2: Copied shapes**

Now let's take the same set of objects and change the relationships around.

In this example an applied shape is created by making a complete copy of a shape template. Here is how a shape is placed on a sheet:

1.  A shape template is selected.

2.  An (x,y) location on the sheet is specified for the shape's center.

3.  A new set of control points is copied from the selected shape template.

4.  An instance of applied shape is created and associated with the new set of control points.

5.  Translation, scale and rotation operations are applied.

Here is the information model for this second example:

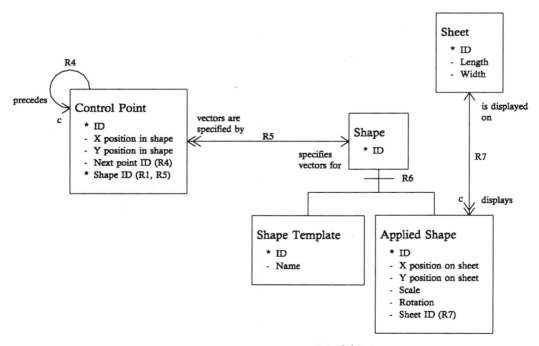

**Model 3.2**

Here are some example instances:

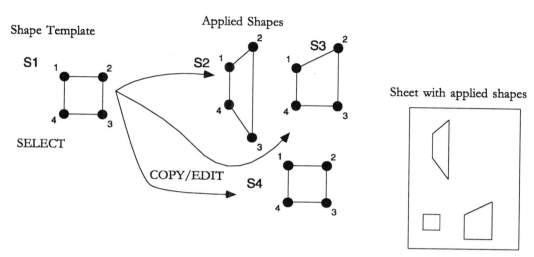

**Figure 3.5**

As before, each applied shape can be translated, rotated and scaled independently. In addition, applied shapes can be independently reshaped. Furthermore, you can edit the control points in the originating shape template (S1) without affecting the generated shapes (S2, S3 and S4).

**Relationships are important**

As you can see, relationships make powerful statements about system policy and behavior. So do objects and attributes, of course, but novice analysts tend to focus on finding and defining objects at the expense of getting the relationships right. Often a client will show me a model that is difficult to complete. Usually the objects are well named and defined, but the relationships aren't even named, let alone defined. Many relationships are missing or are not precise enough. Since relationships define so many of the critical and subtle system policies and behaviors, it is no surprise that skimping on the relationships makes it impossible to arrive at a satisfactory model.

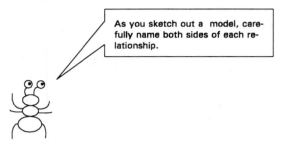

As you sketch out a model, carefully name both sides of each relationship.

The extra time you spend getting the relationships correct (assuming that you are doing all the other analysis tasks - see Chapter 8 on page 143) will always pay off.

# Relationship types

The Shlaer-Mellor information modeling language provides three fundamental relationship types: binary, associative and supertype. Are these three relationship types adequate to model the magnitude and complexity of information in modern software systems?

Assuming for a moment that the answer is yes, consider some benefits to keeping a language symbolically sparse:

- You don't have to memorize much to be able to read a model.

- The rules for translating a model into design elements are simple.

- The model is more transparent - the application rules are highly visible while the internal modeling rules keep a low profile.

- For a given set of requirements, there tends to be only one optimal modeling solution (so you don't get a different model depending on the analyst's mood that day).

The Shlaer-Mellor relationship types are so expressive because they are based on the relational data model. The relational data model draws heavily from set theory, which should readily accommodate any kind of information complexity that we are likely to find. That's about all I understand from an academic perspective. Speaking from experience, I've modeled complex requirements in numerous hightech, real-time, networked, embedded, multiprocessing (add your own impressive, yet meaningless adjectives here) systems. In all these systems, I've never found myself thinking, "Gee, if I just had more relationship types I'd be able to capture these really complex requirements." So the answer to the question I started off with is, "Yes, the three Shlaer-Mellor relationship types are adequate."

**Visualizing relationship types**

One way to appreciate this fact is to visualize the object instances and associations between these instances in each type of relationship. For each relationship type (binary, associative and supertype) I have drawn one or more snapshots of how some example instances are intertwined. This style of illustration is often useful when you are trying to understand exactly how a specific relationship type affects the participating object instances. A quick scan of all the snapshots in the next few pages should give you the sense that these relationship types can harness quite a bit of complexity.

In the coming chapters, each relationship type will be described in detail and its snapshot will be revisited. So, if you aren't already conversant with a particular relationship type, I don't expect you to glance at its snapshot and instantly understand everything. By the time you have finished reading all the relationship chapters in this book, however, you should be able to extract any relationship from one of your own information models and do the visual exercise of drawing an appropriate snapshot.

**Snapshot notation**

Before I move on to the snapshots, let me explain the graphical notation I am using. Take a quick look at Figure 3.1 and you will see icons representing object instances and straight lines representing relationship instances. In the following snapshots I am using generic objects and relationships, so the object instances appear as black dots and the relationship instances appear as arcs between the dots. A set of object instances that belong's to the same object is enclosed in an oblong shape.

# Type 1: Binary Relationships

A *binary relationship* models a correspondence between instances of two different objects or among instances of the same object. If two objects are involved, the relationship is *nonreflexive*.

**Nonreflexive binary relationship: Correspondence between instances of two different objects**

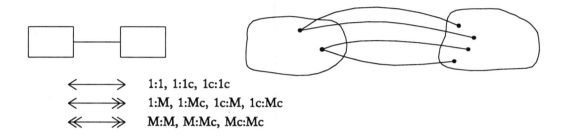

| | |
|---|---|
| ← → | 1:1, 1:1c, 1c:1c |
| ← ⟶≫ | 1:M, 1:Mc, 1c:M, 1c:Mc |
| ≪ ⟶≫ | M:M, M:Mc, Mc:Mc |

**Figure 3.6**

This type of relationship is called binary because it has two perspectives, not because there are two objects involved. A *reflexive* relationship is formed by applying a binary relationship to a single object:

**Binary reflexive relationship: Correspondence among instances of the same object**

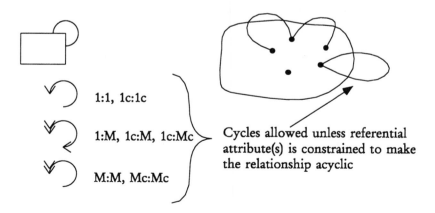

1:1, 1c:1c

1:M, 1c:M, 1c:Mc

M:M, Mc:Mc

Cycles allowed unless referential attribute(s) is constrained to make the relationship acyclic

**Figure 3.7**

**Binary relationships and relationship instances**

It is important to distinguish the concepts of relationship and relationship instance. A *relationship instance* is an association between an instance of one object and

a) an instance of another object or (non-reflexive),

b) an instance of the same object or (reflexive),

c) itself (reflexive).

Here are some relationships and relationship instances:

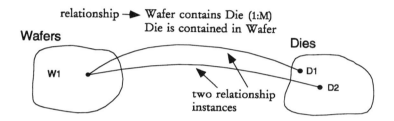

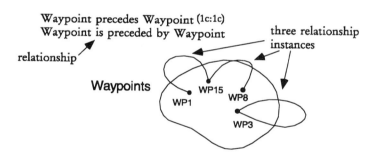

**Figure 3.8**

In the first example in Figure 3.8, there is one relationship (CONTAINS) between the Wafer and Die objects and two relationship instances are shown. The relationship is nonreflexive since it involves more than one object. In the second example, there is one binary reflexive relationship (PRECEDES) on the Waypoint object. Three relationship instances are shown. Notice that one of the instances, WP3, associates with itself. The PRECEDES relationship permits cyclic references. You can make a reflexive relationship acyclic by constraining the appropriate referential attribute (see "Making a relationship acyclic" on page 224).

# Type 2: Associative Relationships

An associative relationship can be built on any binary relationship (including a reflexive binary). Each instance of the binary relationship yields one instance in the associative object if the relationship is (n:n-1) or multiple instances if the relationship is (n:n-M).

**Associative relationship:  Object derived from instance correspondence**

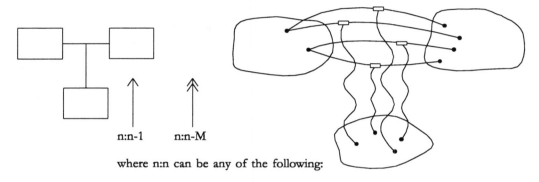

n:n-1          n:n-M

where n:n can be any of the following:

1:1, 1:M, M:M, 1c:1, 1c:1c, 1c:M, 1c:Mc,
M:Mc, Mc:Mc

**Figure 3.9**

# Type 3: Supertype Relationships

The supertype relationship makes it possible to model sets within sets.

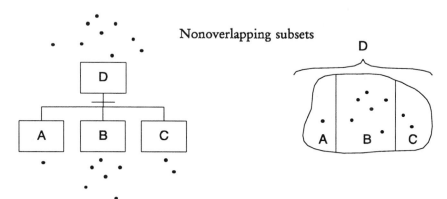

**Figure 3.10**

Or even sets within sets within sets...

**Nonoverlapping, many-layered hierarchical subsets**

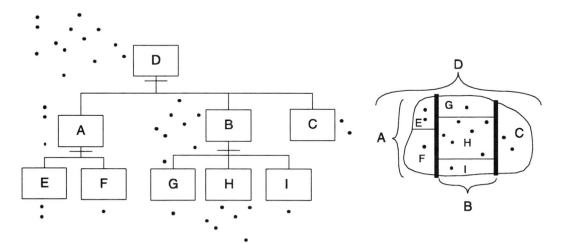

**Figure 3.11**

Multiple supertype relationships can be used to model overlapping subsets.

Overlapping subsets

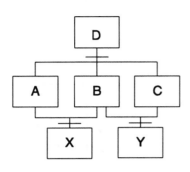 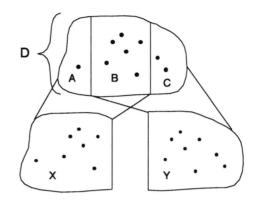

**Figure 3.12**

This type of model is covered in Chapter 7 on page 115.

## And now for some examples

That's it. We can model an enormous variety with just these three types of relationships. In other words, we will model the world in terms of objects that relate to one another, objects that arise out of a relationship, and sets that encompass and intersect one another.

The following chapters use examples to explore these relationship types further.

# Chapter 4        Binary relationships

The fundamental concepts of the binary relationship are multiplicity, conditionality, referential attribute placement and graphic representation. I will start off with some advice on how to think about binary relationships so that you

- don't get instances and abstractions confused,

- build syntactically correct relationships,

- avoid doing stupid things (just kidding).

In addition to listing all possible forms of binary relationship for easy reference, I will detail a few application examples. The nonreflexive form of binary relationship will be examined first with all its variations. Finally, we will review the reflexive form.

**Don't get instances and abstractions confused**

There's a lot more to modeling a binary relationship than drawing an arrow between two objects. To really know what you are doing, you need to consider all the fundamental concepts listed in the introduction to this chapter - not just graphic representation. Furthermore, these concepts must be understood both at the abstract level of objects and relationships *and* at the level of object and relationship instances. Confusion over relationships, especially among novice analysts, arises when the abstract properties of objects and relationships are mixed up with the tangible properties of specific instances.

**How to keep it all straight**

The best way to keep all this stuff straight is to draw your information model on one sheet of paper and then illustrate scenarios involving specific instances on a separate sheet of paper (or on a whiteboard). The graphical information model language is already well defined, but how do you illustrate instances of objects and relationships? There are at least three methods that I like to use, which you will see sprinkled throughout this book: icons, blobs-dots-arcs, and tables. A brief description of each approach follows.

**Icons**

Represent object instances with icons. See Figure 3.1 on page 48 for an example. If you are using a drawing program, build up a clip art library for your project. This clip art, along with increasing skill using the drawing program, will make it possible for you to quickly produce these drawings. If you are drawing on a whiteboard or paper, use your imagination to come up with easy-to-draw[1] icons that clearly represent the intended objects. Relationship instances can be represented various ways. Try connecting lines, relative proximity or containment - one thing inside of another - to convey association.

The downside to the iconic method of instance illustration is that it takes time and effort. This is especially true if you don't have any clip art to work with. The time and effort, however, are rarely wasted. The process of illustrating instances almost always leads you to ask important questions about the application requirements. Critical abstractions often occur to me while I am carefully illustrating a scenario that would not have been apparent if I restricted myself to the other two illustration methods. Besides, you leave a trail of excellent documentation to support your models. I often paste these illustrations into the model descriptions. The illustrations are also indispensable when you present your model to colleagues.

**Blobs, dots and arcs**    If you want to sketch a diagram, but don't like to create icons, then try the approach used in Figure 3.8 on page 57. The advantages and disadvantages of this approach are the opposite of those for the icon illustration method just described. But sometimes you just need a fast sketch.

**Tables**    Finally, there is the table approach demonstrated in Model 4.1. This method of instance illustration is useful when you want to make sure that you aren't breaking any of the table rules. If you can draw instances that conform to good tables, then you can be pretty sure that the corresponding model is syntactically correct. This approach also makes it easy to organize numerous attribute values. The downside of tables is that they make you think too much like a database programmer.[2] Stare at tables too much and you find yourself shuffling attributes around willy-nilly, obsessing about third normal form and, basically, losing sight of the forest for the trees. Okay, you've been warned.

Now let's see what we can do with binary relationships.

---

[1] If you are lazy and have no drawing talent, like me, the trick is to invent an icon that is slightly more descriptive than a circle or square - although that sometimes suffices - which can be quickly drawn.

[2] I can't wait for the e-mail flames.

# Nonreflexive binary relationships

Here again is the snapshot of the nonreflexive binary relationship:

**Nonreflexive binary relationship:  Correspondence between instances of two different objects**

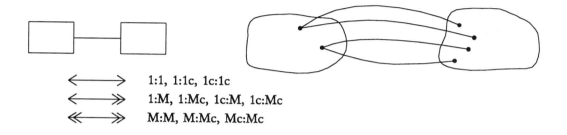

| | |
|---|---|
| ⟵⟶ | 1:1, 1:1c, 1c:1c |
| ⟵⟹ | 1:M, 1:Mc, 1c:M, 1c:Mc |
| ⟸⟹ | M:M, M:Mc, Mc:Mc |

**Figure 4.1**

This snapshot shows what a nonreflexive binary relationship looks like - two objects and a connecting line with arrowheads on each side. The three possible arrow symbols are shown. Next to each arrow symbol is a list of all characteristics that can apply. These characteristics define the multiplicity and the conditionality of the relationship. Finally, the blobs-dots-arcs diagram shows some associations conforming to what a binary relationship might look like (as opposed to an associative or a supertype relationship).

# Multiplicity

The number of instances that can participate on each side of a relationship is called the *multiplicity* of a relationship. The three forms of multiplicity, referential attribute placement and symbology are summarized below:

| Verbal | Graphic | Shorthand text | Where the referential attribute goes |
|---|---|---|---|
| one to one | ←——→ | 1:1 | either side |
| one to many | ←——» | 1:M | M side |
| many to many | «——» | M:M | in an associative object |

**Table 4.1**

These are all unconditional relationship forms. In an unconditional relationship, all instances on both sides of the relationship must participate in at least one association. Let's take a look at an example of each unconditional relationship form.

# One to one

With one-to-one multiplicity, items from each side of the relationship are paired up. Here's an example:

**APPLICATION NOTE**

We have a curve that is moved linearly through space to form an extruded surface. An extruded surface cannot exist independently of its defining curve. A curve is created exclusively for the purpose of creating a surface.

The relationship between Curve and Surface must be 1:1.

Here is a model with some example instances:

Referential attribute on
this side

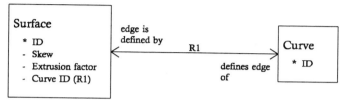

| ID | Skew | Extrusion Factor | Curve ID |
|------|------|------------------|----------|
| S142 | 35 | 1.1 | C17 |
| S102 | 36 | 0.2 | C13 |
| S33 | 12 | 1.8 | C21 |

| ID |
|------|
| C17 |
| C21 |
| C13 |

**Model 4.1**

First, let's look at the table. To implement the 1:1 relationship, we can add a column that references Curve IDs to the table of Surfaces. The only legal values that can be entered in the Surfaces.Curve ID column are defined by the attribute domain of Curve.Curve ID. In the information model, this concept is formalized through the placement of the Curve ID attribute in the Surface object. The attribute domain description of the referential Surface.Curve ID attribute will say "same as the domain of Curve.ID". See "Refer to the original description" on page 196.

We could have done it the other way around:

Referential attribute on this side

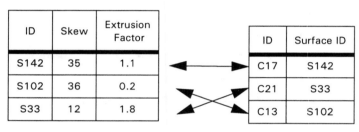

Model 4.2

Either solution is okay, because each solution yields a correct table structure according to the table rules discussed in Chapter 1 on page 3.

## One to many

With one-to-many multiplicity, an item on side A of the relationship may reference multiple items on side B. But an item on side B can relate to only one item on side A. Consider a new application example in which we have a semiconductor wafer with multiple die imprints:

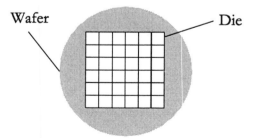

Figure 4.2

To model this relationship, you can place the referenced identifier only in the Die object, because each Die instance can relate to only one Wafer.

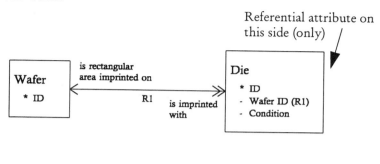

Referential attribute on this side (only)

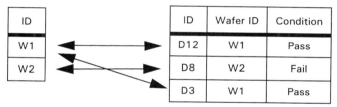

**Model 4.3**

If you try to do it the other way around, you get nonatomic entries that break the table rules.

## Not allowed! This domain is not atomic.

**Model 4.4**

So with a one-to-many, the referential attribute always goes on the side that can reference only one item, as shown in Model 4.3.

# Many to many

With a many-to-many relationship you can't put the referential attribute on either side without breaking the table rules. You have to create a third correlation table as shown in the M:M relationship below:

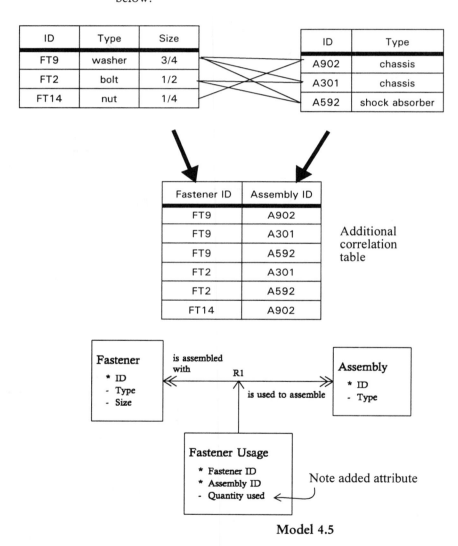

Model 4.5

This correlation table is formalized as an associative object in the information model. After you formalize a M:M relationship, you often find attributes that pertain to the new associative object. In

Model 4.5, Quantity Used refers to the number of Fasteners required in a specific Assembly. For more about associative relationships, see Chapter 5 on page 77.

Is this really an unconditional M:M relationship? That depends on the definitions of Fastener and Assembly. I'm assuming that an Assembly is a device put together with Fasteners. So, by definition, R1 is unconditional on the IS ASSEMBLED WITH side. A Fastener is only of interest, in this particular application, if it is part of an Assembly. Consequently, R1 is also unconditional on the IS USED TO ASSEMBLE side.

# Conditional relationships

In a conditional relationship, instances may exist on specific sides of a relationship that do not participate in any associations. In the following application example, we want to model the usage of cables plugged into sockets.

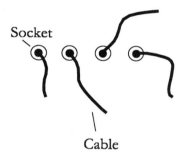

**Figure 4.3**

Only one cable can be accommodated by a socket, and only one socket can be attached to a cable. Both cables and sockets may be unused. Consequently, this is a 1c:1c relationship - conditional on both sides.

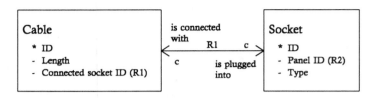

| ID | Length | Connected socket ID |
|----|--------|---------------------|
| C8 | 8′ | S12 |
| C2 | 15′ | S5 |
| C1 | 8′ | None |

| ID | Panel ID | Type |
|----|----------|------|
| S17 | P1 | RCA |
| S12 | P6 | MIDI |
| S5 | P2 | RCA |

**Model 4.6**

To implement this relationship, we can add a column to the Cable table that references the "plugged-in" socket. The only legal values that can be entered in the Connected Socket ID column are defined by the attribute domain of ID in the Sockets table. This concept is formalized by the Connected Socket ID referential attribute in the Cable object. Since the relationship is conditional, the Cable.Connected Socket ID attribute must take on the value "None" when the Cable is unplugged. In the tables above (Model 4.6), Cable C1 is unplugged.

We could have done it the other way around and put the reference column in the Sockets table, as is the case with a 1:1 unconditional relationship. In other words, we could have created a referential attribute called Plugged-in Cable ID in the Socket table that would reference the Cable.ID attribute.

All the unconditional relationship forms can be modified to model conditional relationships.

| Verbal | Graphic | Shorthand | Where the referential attribute goes |
|---|---|---|---|
| one-to-one conditional on one side | ⟵⟶ c | 1:1c | 1c side |
| one-to-one conditional on both sides | ⟵⟶ c  c | 1c:1c | either side |
| one-to-many conditional on the one side | ⟵⟹ c | 1c:M | M side |
| one-to-many conditional on the many side | ⟵⟹ c | 1:Mc | Mc side |
| one-to-many conditional on both sides | ⟵⟹ c  c | 1c:Mc | Mc side |
| many-to-many conditional on one side | ⟸⟹ c | M:Mc | in associative object |
| many-to-many conditional on both sides | ⟸⟹ c  c | Mc:Mc | in associative object |

Table 4.2

For an example of each of these relationships, see Object-Oriented Systems Analysis, S. Shlaer and S. Mellor, Yourdon Press, New York, 1988 (the purple book).

**Where to put the referential attribute**

The referential attribute must be placed in such a way that the table rules are not broken. This means that you never place the referential attribute opposite a many (M) side.

First, use the multiplicity of the relationship to determine on which side to place the referential attribute. For conditional relationships, try to put the referential attribute on the conditional side (the same side as the little c). If the relationship is conditional on both sides, then, regardless of multiplicity, you are probably best off with an associative object. You will almost always find descriptive attributes that belong in that associative object.

If you place an attribute opposite a 1c side, then sometimes the attribute value will be "None". You must ensure that the attribute domain definition includes the "None" value. See "Refer to the original description" on page 196 for an example.

# Reflexive relationships

A reflexive relationship works exactly like a nonreflexive relationship except that you have only one object. All principles of multiplicity, conditionality and referential attribute placement work the same way for nonreflexive and reflexive relationships. Even so, the reflexive relationship can stir up a little confusion. This happens mostly because abstractions and instances get mixed up. If you get confused, it helps to draw an instance illustration and apply all the same rules that work for nonreflexive relationships.

Let's review the snapshot of the reflexive relationship:

**Binary reflexive relationship: Correspondence among instances of the same object**

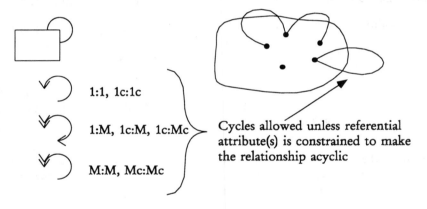

1:1, 1c:1c

1:M, 1c:M, 1c:Mc

M:M, Mc:Mc

Cycles allowed unless referential attribute(s) is constrained to make the relationship acyclic

**Figure 4.4**

This snapshot shows what a reflexive binary relationship looks like - one object and a connecting line with arrowheads on one side or on both sides. The three possible arrow symbols are shown. Next to each arrow symbol is a list of all characteristics that can apply. Notice that not all combinations of multiplicity and conditionality are possible. The blobs-dots-arcs diagram shows some associations among the instances of a single object.

**When to use a reflexive relationship**

Reflexive relationships are necessary when you want to model a relationship among instances of the same object. Consider a script containing a set of commands to be executed in sequence.

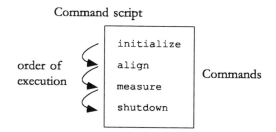

**Figure 4.5**

The order of command execution is a relationship among instances of only one object, the Command object. This can be seen when you take the perspective of two associated instances of Command. Take the second and third Commands from the top in Figure 4.5 - `align` and `measure`. The `align` Command IS EXECUTED BEFORE the `measure` command and the `measure` Command IS EXECUTED AFTER the `align` Command. Q: How many Commands can be executed after[1] `align`? A: One - at most. Q: How many Commands can be executed before `measure`? A: One - at most. Consequently, we have a one-to-one biconditional (1c:1c) relationship on the Command object as illustrated below:

---

[1]In a reflexive relationship, when I say "after", I mean "directly after". This is one of those things that should be spelled out in the relationship description.

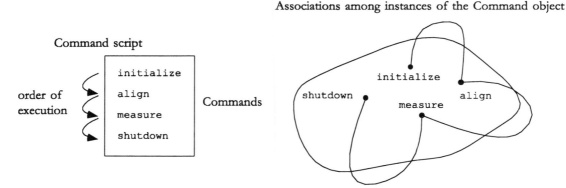

Associations among instances of the Command object

Command script

order of execution

Commands

Binary relationship applied to a single object

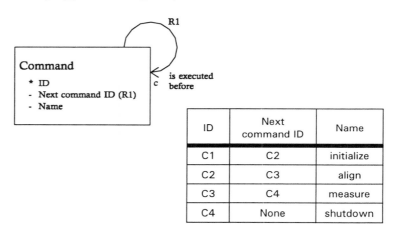

| ID | Next command ID | Name |
|----|----|----|
| C1 | C2 | initialize |
| C2 | C3 | align |
| C3 | C4 | measure |
| C4 | None | shutdown |

**Figure 4.6**

An additional identifier attribute is necessary since we don't want to preclude another Command of the same type within a single script. At this point you might ask, "Why not just number the identifier values to reflect the command order?" Not in a Shlaer-Mellor table you don't!

**Why a sequence can't be numbered**

You cannot place entries in the order of execution because instance order is *insignificant* in a table. That's one of our fundamental table rules. Object instances can be related only through the use of referential attributes. If you numbered the IDs, what would happen when you insert and delete Commands? You would have to renumber them. By sticking to referential attributes, we never have to think about special strategies when we add or remove instances.

**How to formalize a reflexive relationship**

We formalize a reflexive 1c:1c relationship the same way that we formalize a nonreflexive 1c:1c relationship. In a nonreflexive relationship (see page 63), we add an attribute on one side of the relationship that references the object on the other side. But since we only have one object in a reflexive relationship, we must put the referential attribute in the same object. In Figure 4.6, Command.Next Command ID references Command.ID. The contents of the Commands table demonstrates how this works for specific instances. Notice that Command instance C4 has "None" in it's Next Command ID column since it is the last Command to be executed. Alternatively, R1 could be formalized by making the relationship associative and placing Next Command ID in the associative object. This would remove the need to account for a "None" value.

**Graphic representation of reflexive relationships**

When all the instances are in the same object, asymmetric conditionality (1:1c and M:Mc) doesn't have any meaning. If you say that a relationship is reflexive 1c:1c, then you have some kind of a sequence, list or other linear ordering. The conditionality accounts for the head and tail of the ordering. If the relationship is (1:1) then the head and tail must always be joined. This gives you a linear and circular ordering. But what could (1:1c) mean? Since the relationship is applied to a single object, you have no way to distinguish the instances on one side of the relationship from those on the other side. Consequently, the relationship symbol has an arrow on only one side. This notation reflects the fact that there are no (1:1c) and (M:Mc) reflexive relationships. When the multiplicity is one to many, however, asymmetric conditionality (1c:M, 1:Mc) is meaningful. This is because the referential attribute can refer to only one side of the relationship, which precludes any ambiguity. So these reflexive relationships do have an arrow on each side of the relationship symbol.

**More examples**

Well, that's it for the basics. I could write whole chapters on how reflexive relationships work and how you can use them. In fact - I did. Part 3 contains several chapters on reflexive relationships.

# Chapter 5

# Associative relationships

The associative object was described in Chapter 1, as a way of formalizing a many-to-many relationship. An *associative relationship* is simply a binary relationship that is formalized with an associative object. Associative relationships might seem a little confusing at first. How the instances in an associative object correlate with the participating instances on either side of its binary relationship might not be clear. You might be wondering when you should make binary relationships, especially one-to-one relationships, associative. A few examples should help.

Let's create an associative relationship by extending a simple binary relationship. First the application...

APPLICATION NOTE

A flot is a flat optical device used in fiber-optic memory systems. We use a laser to inspect various physical and optical properties of flots.

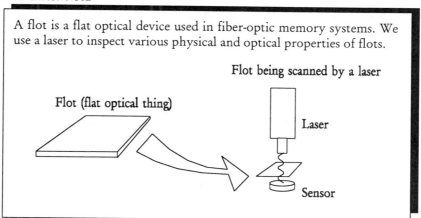

Figure 5.1

We can model the fact that a flot is being scanned by a laser illuminator with a nonassociative binary relationship:

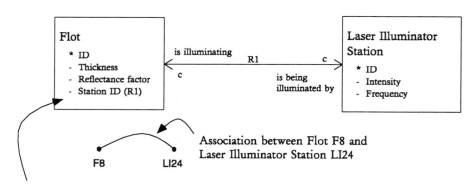

For instance F8, Flot.Station ID = LI24

**Model 5.1**

**Creating a nonassociative relationship instance**

To create a relationship instance in a nonassociative binary relationship, you set the value of a referential attribute. In Model 5.1 an instance of Flot (F8) is associated with an instance of Laser Illuminator Station (LI24). This is accomplished by setting the Station ID for F8 to the value LI24.

**Creating an associative relationship instance**

To create a relationship instance in an associative relationship, you create an object instance in the associative object:

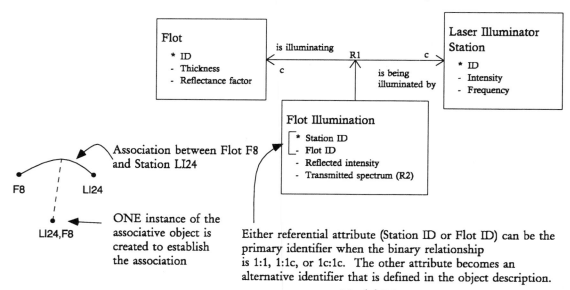

Association between Flot F8 and Station LI24

ONE instance of the associative object is created to establish the association

Either referential attribute (Station ID or Flot ID) can be the primary identifier when the binary relationship is 1:1, 1:1c, or 1c:1c. The other attribute becomes an alternative identifier that is defined in the object description.

**Model 5.2**

In Model 5.2, an instance of Flot (F8) is associated with an instance of Laser Illuminator Station (LI24), just as before. To establish the association, an instance of Flot Illumination is created. This new object instance has its Station ID set to LI24 and its Flot ID set to F8. Since this is a one-to-one relationship, either Station ID or Flot ID will suffice as the identifier. Notice, also, that the associative object has some new attributes that describe the relationship (as opposed to the objects on either side of the relationship). This often happens when you make a binary relationship associative.

**Why create an associative object?**

Okay, so you have two choices when it comes to formalizing a binary relationship. Choice 1: Keep the relationship nonassociative and stick a referential attribute in one of the participating objects.[1] Choice 2: Make the relationship associative, model an associative object, and stick the referential attribute(s) in it. Which choice is best? It might help to rephrase the question: Why would you want to create an instance of an object each time a relationship instance is established in a binary relationship?

Here are three reasons:

**Multiplicity**

1. The multiplicity on each side of the binary relationship is M. Since you can't place a referential attribute opposite an M side without violating the table rules, you need a third object to contain the referential attributes.

**Assign attributes to a relationship**

2. Attributes in addition to those necessary to formalize the binary relationship are generated only when an association is established in the binary relationship. Here's an example:

---

[1] That's just one object if we are talking about a reflexive relationship.

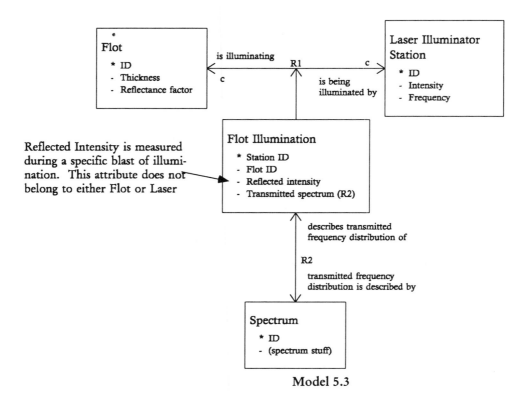

**Model 5.3**

Here, Reflected Intensity and Transmitted Spectrum are relevant only when a Flot is being Illuminated.

|  |  |
|---|---|
| **Model the behavior of a relationship** | 3. Special behavior comes into play whenever an association is established in the binary relationship. This behavior has more to do with the associative object than it does with the objects on either side of the relationship. |

Where, for example, is the best place to describe the dynamics of the Flot Illumination test process? In the Flot Illumination state model! The life cycle probably goes like this: INITIATING ILLUMINATION ➔ WAITING FOR LASER TO WARM UP ➔ ILLUMINATING ➔ WAITING FOR DATA COLLECTION TO COMPLETE ➔ SHUTTING DOWN LASER ➔ TERMINATING ILLUMINATION... or something like that.

Since the multiplicity of this relationship is one-to-one, you *could* cram all the attributes, relationships and behavior into the Flot or the Laser Illuminator Station and end up with a syntactically correct object model. So what? That makes the model less descriptive and extendable. The goal of analysis is to expose information - not to hide it!

# Multiplicity on associative relationships

**Single associative multiplicity**

Two kinds of multiplicity apply to associative relationships. Most of the time the multiplicity is one. That is, for every association in a binary relationship, one instance is generated in the corresponding associative object. The Flot IS BEING ILLUMINATED BY Laser Illuminator Station relationship was first cast as a 1c:1c binary relationship and then it was recast as a single associative 1-(1c:1c) relationship. The "1-" in the 1-(n:n) notation indicates that one instance is created in the associative object for each binary association. In the graphic notation, the "1-" is designated by the single arrowhead on the associative relationship symbol.

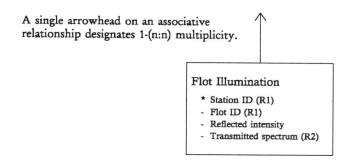

A single arrowhead on an associative relationship designates 1-(n:n) multiplicity.

**Flot Illumination**

* Station ID (R1)
- Flot ID (R1)
- Reflected intensity
- Transmitted spectrum (R2)

**Model 5.4**

**Many associative multiplicity**

It is also possible to construct an associative relationship in which each binary association yields multiple instances in the corresponding associative object. In this case, the multiplicity is denoted as M-(n:n), and a double arrowhead appears on the associative relationship symbol.

Let's look at an application example:

APPLICATION NOTE

In a material transport system, parts must be delivered to work stations for assembly. (These work stations are called Assembly Stations). We need to track the progress of each part delivery as it makes its way through the factory. Depending on the location where a part is stored, it may be delivered via conveyor belt, automated guided vehicle, robot or through some combination. Parts are delivered in special purpose boxes. Every box has a unique bar code label.

If the quantity of a part requested exceeds the capacity of a single box, multiple boxes may be used to complete the delivery of the part order. These boxes will be routed through the factory independently.

Here is an example part delivery scenario:

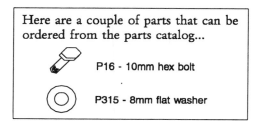

Boxes of parts enroute to assembly site AS5

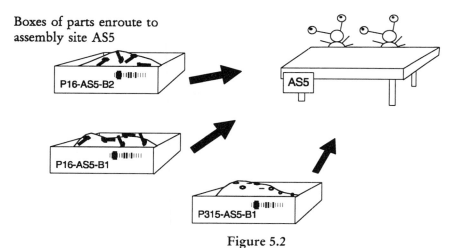

Figure 5.2

In this scenario, an order for part number P16 (10mm hex bolts) is being delivered in two boxes. A separate order for P315 (8mm flat washers) is being delivered in a single box. Both orders are on their way to Assembly Station AS5.

Now let's look at the associative object model that formalizes part deliveries:

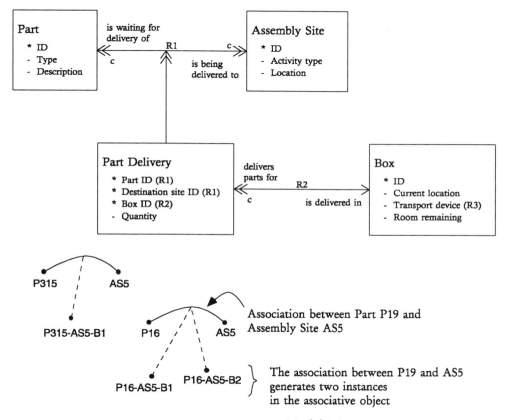

Model 5.5

The IS DELIVERED TO relationship (R1) is M-(Mc:Mc). One or more instances may be created in the Part Delivery for each association between a Part instance and an Assembly Site instance. Consequently, Part ID + Assembly Site ID are not sufficient to distinguish these multiple associative object instances. Since each Part Delivery is unconditionally associated with a Box, we can use the Box ID referential attribute to complete the identifier for Part Delivery.

Alternatively, we could make a single attribute identifier for Part Delivery called Part Delivery.ID, which we could number PD1, PD2, and so on. Then Part ID + Assembly ID + Box ID would become an alternative identifier, which would not be marked on the information model graphic.

**Decomposing a many associative**

You can decompose any M-(n:n) relationship into a 1-(n:n) relationship by adding an extra object and 1:M relationship to the associative object like so:

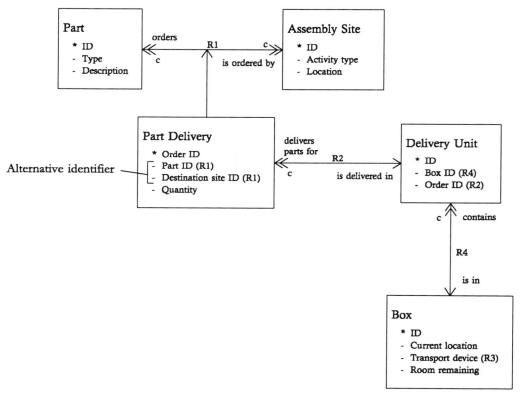

**Model 5.6**

Here's what changed:

- R1 was redefined as the 1-(Mc:Mc) IS ORDERED BY relationship.

- The associative object is redefined in accordance with the relationship - now it is a Part Order.

- A 1:M relationship (R4) is added that connects Part Order to the new Delivery Unit object.

**Decompose M-(n:n) relationships**  In general, I try to decompose all M-(n:n) into 1-(n:n) relationships. Model 5.6 separates the concept of a Part Order from a Delivery Unit. This will make it possible to express subtle policy differences that may arise involving either of these objects. Let's say that we get a new type of Box that is partitioned into Bins. A Bin must contain Parts associated with a single Part Order. We would then want to model the relationship between Delivery Unit and Bin. Model 5.6 could easily be extended to handle this new requirement. If we were using Model 5.5, we would have a little more work to do. Also, Model 5.6 is easier for most people to interpret at first glance.

# Conditionality on associative relationships

It is a common mistake to put a **c** on the associative relationship arrow as shown in Model 5.7 below. But it doesn't make any sense!

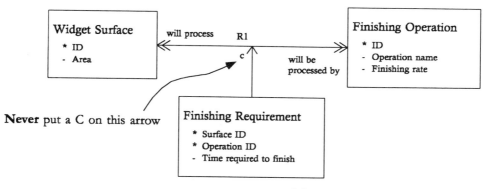

**Model 5.7**

You can express all the conditionality you need by placing **c**'s only on the two sides of the binary relationship. Consider this application:

APPLICATION NOTE

> In a factory, widget surfaces are prepared with various processes such as buffing, filing and sanding. These are called finishing operations. Before a widget surface is prepared, a manufacturing engineer must select a set of predefined finishing operations. (For this example we don't need to worry about sequencing of operations). Only those surfaces that will contact other machine parts must be prepared. These are called contact surfaces.

**Conditionality on one side**  By definition, all Contact Surfaces require at least one Finishing Operation. Since Finishing Operations are predefined, the WILL BE PROCESSED BY relationship is conditional on the Contact Surface side. We can model it as a 1-(M:Mc) associative relationship as shown:

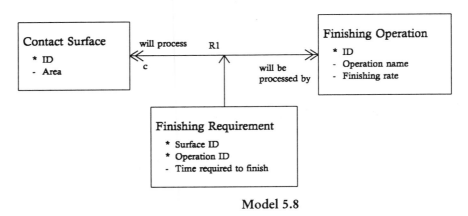

**Model 5.8**

Some example instances of these objects are sketched below:

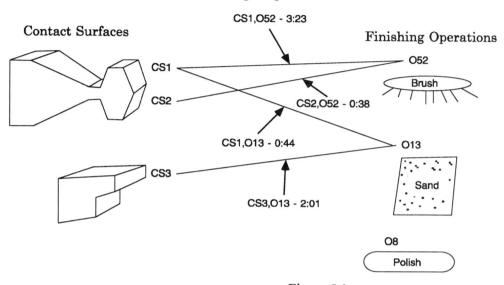

**Figure 5.3**

Model 5.8 says that each Contact Surface requires at least one Finishing Operation. But a Finishing Operation might be defined that is currently not required by any Contact Surface (O8 - Polish, for example). No problem; O8 just sits there. Since O8 does not associate with any instance of Contact Surface, no Finishing Requirement is created. But for every associative object instance, there must exist a corresponding Contact Surface and Operation.

**Conditionality on both sides**

For the sake of exploring conditionality in associative relationships, let's make our model a little less precise. The Contact Surface object is replaced in the model below with the more encompassing Widget Surface object. Any surface on a Widget, including a Contact Surface, is a Widget Surface. Consequently, we have to add another **c** to relationship R1 making it 1-(Mc:Mc). Not all Widget Surfaces require Finishing Operations.

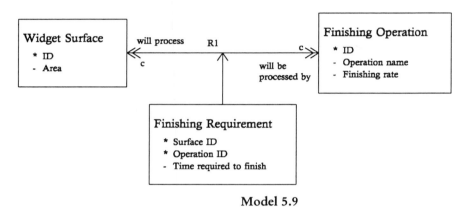

**Model 5.9**

Now our sketch needs to be altered a little bit...

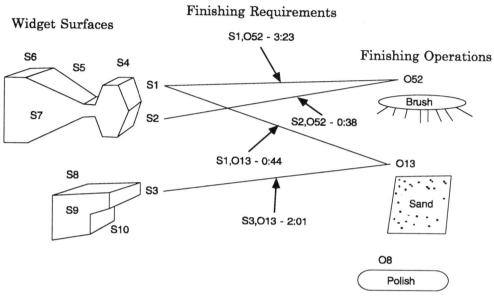

**Figure 5.4**

Even though the conditionality of the binary relationship has changed, an instance of Finishing Requirement still must exist for each association between an instance of Widget Surface and an instance of Finishing Operation. If a Widget Surface does not require a Finishing Operation, S9 for example, it just sits there, and no Finishing Requirement is created.

To sum up, conditionality on associative relationships is tweaked using only the **c**'s on either side of the binary relationship. You can't create an instance of an associative object without establishing a corresponding association between instances on both sides of the binary relationship. So it makes no sense to put a **c** on the associative object arrow.

# Frequently asked questions about associative relationships

**Shouldn't there be a diamond on associative relationships?**

No. You might find diamonds in old Shlaer-Mellor object models. The diamond notation was initially borrowed from the Chen[1] entity relationship diagram notation.

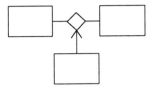

It eventually became apparent that the diamond symbol did not convey any information. Diamonds are chart junk.

**Can more than three objects participate in an associative relationship?**

Can several objects all come together to create one big associative object?

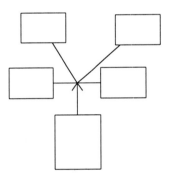

Theoretically, yes. But you have to set up the identifiers so that all of the attribute dependency rules described in Chapters 1 and 2 are satisfied. In the unlikely event that you do this without making an attribute dependency error somewhere, the resulting model will probably have several problems: The associative relationship will be difficult to interpret. The whole thing will fall apart as soon as any of the relevant application requirements change. The effort to bind all the relationships together will probably cause subtle application policies to be overlooked. When presented with a three or four way associative relationship, I have never had difficulty finding an overlooked application issue that causes the whole mess to unravel.

---

[1]Peter Chen, *The Entity-Relationship Approach to Logical Data Base Design*, Q.E.D. Information Sciences, Wellesley, Massachusetts, 1977.

You can model all the complexity you like without resorting to associative relationships involving more than one binary relationship. Besides, there is no point in hiding lots of interesting application requirements by snarling them into a single association. The goal of analysis is to expose information - not hide it.

**Do I put R's on the identifiers in the associative object?**

No. The referential attributes that form the identifier of an associative object are, by convention, not marked with (R)'s. It's a convenient shorthand. It won't hurt if you decide to put the R's on anyway. In any case, you must define the referential properties of all attributes in the attribute and relationship descriptions.

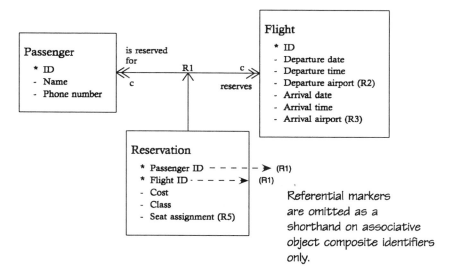

**How do I name an associative object?**

I try to make the name of the relationship match up with the name of the object (or vice versa). If you end up with a nonsensical name for either the relationship or the associative object, then you may need to rethink the relationship.

*Chapter 6*

# Basic supertype relationships

I've seen the supertype relationship used in some pretty strange ways. By "strange" I mean both unproductive and syntactically incorrect. This is due to a common lack of understanding in a couple of key areas. Sometimes the underlying sets and subsets of object instances are not properly visualized. Other times the way the set concepts are properly formalized is unclear. Even if all this is understood, it is easy to spin a tangled web of relationships (supertype and otherwise) that obfuscate rather than expose the true application requirements. Having made plenty of these mistakes myself, I appreciate the need to cut through all this confusion. I hope the next two chapters help!

In this chapter we will start with a snapshot diagram of the supertype relationship that illustrates the underlying set concepts. Next we take a look at two common problems that the supertype relationship neatly solves. Then we construct some tables, fill them in with instances, and correlate the instances to see how the supertype relationship is formalized. Finally, we will compare two different strategies for creating and maintaining identifier values for all the instances in a supertype relationship.

**Supertype or subtype?** But first, let's get our terms straight. The supertype relationship is sometimes referred to as a subtype relationship or a super/subtype relationship. When you can't get one to work, various unprintable names also come to mind, but let's not worry about that now. For consistency's sake, I will always use the term *supertype* relationship.

## What is a supertype relationship?

By definition, all the instances of an object share the same characteristics and behavior. This strict definition will lead us to model two similar, but slightly different, things in separate objects. In an air traffic control system, Planes and Helicopters both have Altitude, Airspeed and Heading attributes. They each take off, fly and land. But Planes require runways and Helicopters don't. This small difference leads us

93

to create the separate objects Plane and Helicopter. Otherwise, our system wouldn't be smart enough to let a Helicopter take off even though all runways are busy.

But our system should also be smart enough to recognize the similarities between Planes and Helicopters. This leads us to model a single object called Aircraft. All instances of Aircraft share the same characteristics and behavior if we define Aircraft as any vehicle that flies.

**What the supertype relationship does**

The supertype relationship makes it possible to say that Planes and Helicopters are different and yet are the same to the extent that they are Aircraft.

> WARNING: If you program in an object-oriented language, you are probably thinking at this point; "Oh yeah, that's just inheritance." Wrong. Wrong. Wrong. The concepts are seductively similar, yet just different enough to get you into endless trouble. It's sort of like the trouble you would get into if you were trying to lose weight and got the concept of bagels and donuts confused. The differences aren't just accidental, either, they are quite intentional. Inheritance is an excellent implementation mechanism often used to translate supertype relationships into good object-oriented code. In fact, you can use inheritance to implement some nonsupertype relationships also - 1:M binaries, for example. (I'm not saying that you should, but you could). Anyway, I recommend that you put everything you know about inheritance in a little box and hide it under the desk while you absorb these next two chapters.

The supertype relationship establishes one object as the supertype object. In our air traffic example, Aircraft would be the supertype. Each potential instance of Aircraft is then categorized into exactly one subtype object. Plane and Helicopter are the subtype objects. This is how the relationship is designated on the information model:

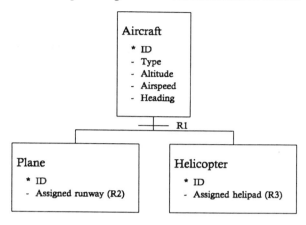

**Model 6.1**

This model says that every instance of Aircraft is either a Plane or a Helicopter. It also says that every instance of Helicopter is an Aircraft and every instance of Plane is an Aircraft. Each instance of Helicopter, consequently, has its own set of values corresponding to the attributes in Aircraft and so does each instance of Plane. The crossbar symbol is always closest to the supertype object.

Imagine a set of Aircraft instances that includes a mix of Helicopters and Planes. The supertype relationship completely partitions the set of all Aircraft instances into two distinct subsets - the set of Planes and the set of Helicopters. Conversely, you could say that the union of the set of Planes and Helicopters constitutes the complete set of Aircraft instances (at any given point in time).

The following snapshot summarizes how the supertype relationship makes it possible to model completely partitioned sets of generic instances:

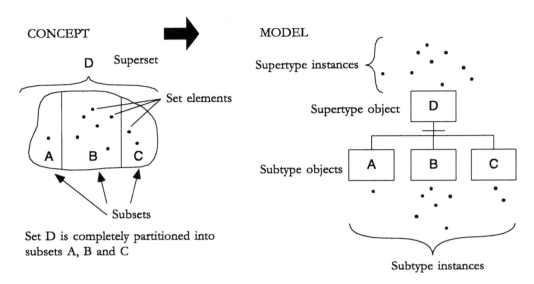

**Figure 6.1**

The left-hand side of Figure 6.1 illustrates the underlying set concepts. On the right we see how these concepts are realized in a supertype relationship. The rules are summarized below:

**Set partitioning**   **Set**: A superset is completely partitioned into nonoverlapping subsets.

**Model**: The supertype object models the superset and each subtype object models a subset.

**Set membership**   **Set**: Each element of a subset (A, B or C) is simultaneously a member of the superset D.

**Model**:

- Each subtype instance from A, B or C has exactly one corresponding supertype instance in D.

- Each supertype instance in D must have exactly one corresponding instance in ONE of the subtype objects (A, B, or C).

- If you create an instance of D, you must also create an instance in A, B or C. If you create an instance in A, B or C, you must also create an instance in D. If you delete an instance of D, you must also delete the corresponding subtype instance. If you delete an instance in A, B or C, you must delete the corresponding instance in D.

# When to use supertype relationships

Before diving deeper into the methodology to see how the supertype relationship is formalized, let's first look at some examples of where it is useful.

There are two different situations where the supertype relationship becomes necessary:

1.  Generalization and specialization

2.  Mutual exclusion

# Generalization and specialization

The following application presents a problem in which a number of general rules are stated along with some important exceptions. We have an analysis goal and a modeling goal. The analysis goal is to formulate a small set of concepts and rules that take into account both the general rules and the specific exceptions. The modeling goal is to formalize these concepts and rules into an information model. First, let's take a look at the application.

We are creating a user interface for a diagnostic medical scanner.

A variety of parameters, like operator name, scan frequency, focal depth, and power setting, can be input and edited using a joystick and/or a keyboard. We want to prevent the entry of illegal values, although for some parameters it doesn't matter what you enter. String parameters, for example, can be assigned any arbitrary ASCII string. Numeric parameters, on the other hand, must be real numbers, which may or may not be constrained.

In the unconstrained case, a continuous range of numeric values is acceptable within a virtually[1] infinite range. To avoid a divide-by-zero condition, a zero value is illegal for some numeric parameters. Another example is the Frequency Scale parameter, which can take on all numeric values other than -1 and 1 (don't ask me why).

Due to the nature of this medical device, we don't ever want to force the user to resort to the keyboard for data entry. In fact, we must do whatever we can to make the joystick the preferred method of data entry. Since the magnitude of legal numeric ranges varies considerably, we will let the user specify a joystick increment speed for each numeric parameter. Furthermore, the user may want some values to wrap around when the joystick hits the upper or lower range limit, or the user might want to stop incrementing when a limit is reached.

Some numeric parameters specify discrete settings. In this case only integers may be entered. The filter setting, for example, must be an integer in the range from 1 to 5.

There are also some toggle settings. The Invert Video parameter must be either True or False. Question: what do we do about the Background Texture, which has three values: Smooth, Rough or None?

The parameter names and editing constraints are configured by the system developers for each application parameter.

---

[1] Well, to the extent that the implementation platform can accommodate us. The application does not specify or require a limit.

The first step is to account for all these rules, along with any anticipated rules, using as few concepts as possible. After some analysis, we end up with a technical note that defines a scheme for defining parameter domains. Here is the key illustration taken from that note:

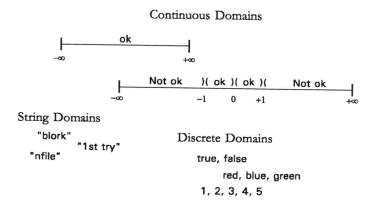

**Figure 6.2**

The different types of parameters have been grouped according to editing constraints. Since there is virtually no constraint on the entry of string values, string domains constitute one group. Continuous parameter domains can be constrained by marking off ranges on a number line. A variable joystick increment speed will be associated with this type of parameter. Finally, we define discrete parameter domains as an ordered list of acceptable values. The list order represents the sequence in which values are displayed when the joystick is pushed in either direction. Discrete domains account for toggles and small lists of numeric and nonnumeric values. A long list of integers (0 to 9999) would be handled using a continuous parameter domain along with a precision modifier, set appropriately.

Now we can build a supertype relationship that formalizes these different parameter domains:

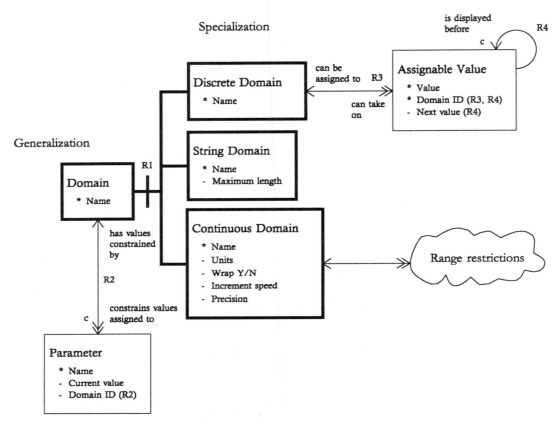

**Model 6.2**

This model says that every Parameter is defined by a single domain which must be Discrete, String or Continuous. A Discrete Domain consists of a list of values that can be assigned to a Parameter. No restrictions are placed on a String Domain. Our model takes into account a number of properties (Units, Wrap, Increment Speed and Precision) that apply only to continuous parameters. But we have yet to model the actual mechanism for restricting illegal number ranges. (And we won't, since that takes us beyond the scope of supertype relationships).

To better visualize how the supertype solution works, let's look at some example instances:

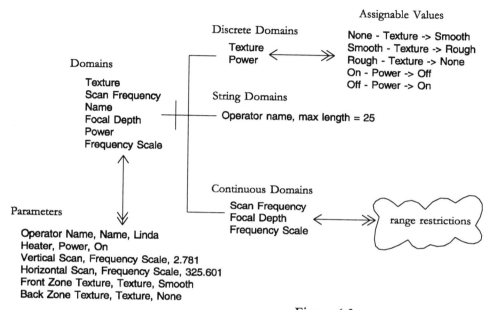

**Figure 6.3**

As you can see, all the cases mentioned in the application note are handled (or can be readily handled) by Model 6.1. First we had to separate the concept of a Parameter from the concept of a Domain. The Domain object represents a set of rules for assigning values. The Parameter object represents a control value that is constrained according to the rules of a Domain. The Texture Domain, for example, permits the assignment of the values None, Smooth and Rough. The Front Zone Texture and Back Zone Texture Parameters are constrained by the Texture Domain. In Figure 6.3, the Front Zone Texture Parameter is currently set to Smooth while the Back Zone Texture Parameter is set to None.

All Domains are the same in that they constrain one or more Parameters. But each of the three types of Domains uses different rules to constrain the set of legal values. Discrete Domains specify an enumeration of Assignable Values. These Assignable Values are organized into a display sequence so that when a user moves the joystick or hits an arrow key, the next sequenced value will be presented. String Domains simply constrain the length of the entered string. Continuous Domains are defined in terms of a system of range restrictions hinted at, but not modeled.

Specialization and generalization are the most common uses of supertyping.

**Specialization**   Use supertyping for specialization when

- you have an object where behavior is the same for all instances, but there are some minor (and sometimes major) exceptions.

- certain attributes change or lose meaning as an object changes state.

- certain relationships are systematically formed or broken as an object changes state.

**Generalization**   Use supertyping for generalization when

- one or more attributes with the same name keep popping up in seemingly disparate objects.[1]

- one or more relationships (referential attributes) with the same name keep popping up in seemingly disparate objects.

Now let's take a look at a completely different way to use the supertype relationship.

# Mutual exclusion

The supertype relationship breaks a set into mutually exclusive subsets. This concept comes in handy when you are faced with application requirements that call for an EXCLUSIVE OR type of situation.

---

[1]In an animation system, for example, coordinate attributes X, Y kept appearing in different objects. So we abstracted a supertype object where we placed/promoted the ubiquitous attributes. Ultimately, however, this supertyping led us to discover a whole new problem domain that dealt expressly with coordinate motion.

A scanner has a sensor that acquires a lot of data. This data is fed through various processing stages which are implemented in hardware. Due to application requirements and the way the hardware is designed, you have to make careful choices about how you route the data.

Here is one example: You can feed the data through one of the high-frequency analyzers or you can feed it through a decimator. To increase bandwidth, it is sometimes necessary to use multiple frequency analyzers or decimators in parallel. But it is extremely important to never perform both decimation and high frequency analysis simultaneously.

Let's take a look at the objects involved:

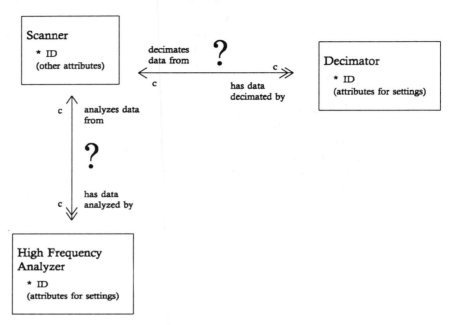

**Model 6.3**

There is no way that any combination of binary relationships and objects can express the desired application rules. We can model a Scanner connected to many Decimators and High Frequency Analyzers, but we can't exclude the possibility of being hooked up to a combination of the two.

That's where the supertype relationship comes in...

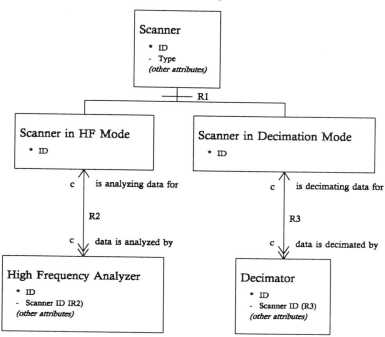

**Model 6.4**

As you can see, a Scanner must now be placed in one of two modes before linking up to any data-processing hardware. This makes it impossible to mix High Frequency Analyzers and Decimators in the same Scanner output path.

**More exclusion**     For a different type of problem that requires supertype exclusion, see Chapter 13 on page 209.

# How supertypes are formalized

Like all relationship types, supertype relationships are formalized using tables and referential attributes. Here is a small example application.

APPLICATION NOTE

A machine that cuts machine parts can be operated manually or automatically. In manual mode a laser is guided through each cut. In automatic mode an entire part is cut using a predefined pattern.

We can compare the supertype relationship to a binary relationship which we already know how to formalize:

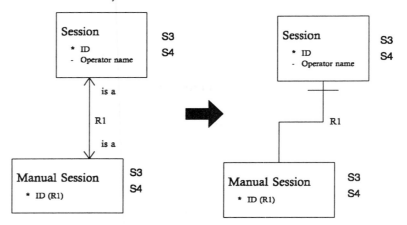

**Model 6.5**

The construct on the right is never used in practice, because it is essentially the same as a 1:1 relationship. I drew this example to show that a referential attribute can formalize the supertype just like a 1:1 relationship. In both cases the referential attribute can be placed on either side of the relationship.

If we try to extend the 1:1 relationship to accommodate another sub-type...

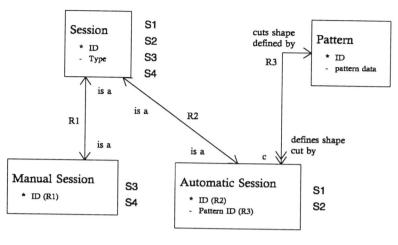

**Model 6.6**

...it doesn't work, because a Session IS EITHER a Manual Session OR an Automatic Session. The two unconditional relationships drawn above, taken together, say IS BOTH, not IS EITHER. If we make R1 and R2 conditional, then we end up with an indecisive MIGHT BE.

As demonstrated with the medical scanner example, we want each supertype instance to correspond to exactly one subtype instance, and vice versa.

We can't get this result with any combination of binary relationships. It is possible, however, to construct Shlaer-Mellor tables that model mutually exclusive subsets. Here they are:

**Session**

| ID | Operator name |
|----|---------------|
| S3 | phil |
| S4 | susan |
| S2 | phil |
| S1 | zog |

**Manual Session**

| ID |
|----|
| S3 |
| S4 |

**Automatic Session**

| ID | Pattern ID |
|----|------------|
| S2 | PAT7 |
| S1 | PAT35 |

**Figure 6.4**

The supertype relationship can be visualized by an arrangement of tables like those shown above. The table on top is a superset of all object instances in the supertype relationship, and the following tables contain instances of nonoverlapping subsets.

So far we have a graphic notation and the right instances in the right tables. But how do we ensure that the super- and subtype instances correlate?

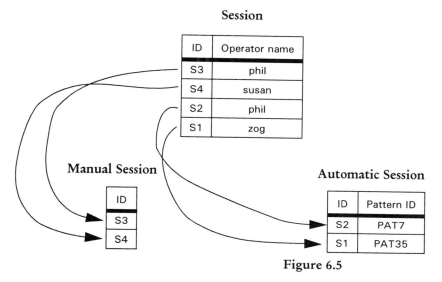

Figure 6.5

After all, this is an IS A relationship, so super- and subtype instances are bound together pretty tightly.

# Supertype identifier policies

We need a clear policy for creating instances, assigning identifier values and placing referential attributes so that we don't end up with any orphaned instances.

Actually, there are at least two policies based on where the creation of new instances is initiated: in the supertype or in the subtypes.

**Policy 1: Instances are born in the supertype (trickle down)**

With this policy, all instances originate in the supertype and trickle down into the appropriate subtype. To see how this works, let's create a new instance of Manual Session. First, we need to create an instance of Session that will assign a new Session.ID value to the instance. It turns out to be S5. We set the Session.Type attribute to Type=MANUAL. Now we tell the Manual Session object to create a new instance using the supplied identifier value ID=S5. The new instance is created, and Manual Session.ID (S5) is both the identifier of Manual Session and a reference to the corresponding Session instance.

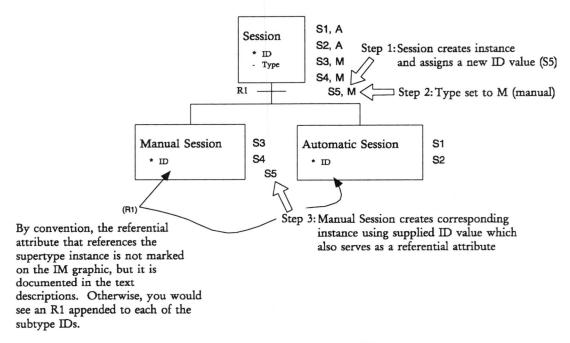

Model 6.7

Since the supertype is responsible for numbering all the instances and since each subtype holds a subset of those instances, a duplicate ID cannot be generated.

Compare this policy with the next one, in which the subtypes generate the ID values.

**Policy 2: Instances are born in the subtypes (percolation)**

You can generate instances and identifier values local to each subtype object that percolate up into the supertype object. Again, let's create an instance of Manual Session - this time in the Manual Session object first. We create an instance of Manual Session and assign a locally unused identifier value, which turns out to be S3. Now we pass this value along to the supertype. To prevent a collision with a potential S3 Automatic Session, a suffix is tacked on to produce S3-M. The suffix is stored in the Session.Type attribute which is part of Session's compound identifier.

By convention, the referential attribute that references the supertype instance is not marked on the schematic, but it is documented in the text descriptions. Otherwise, you would see an (R1) appended to the supertype ID.

The attribute domain of Session.ID is defined as the union of all the subtype ID attribute domains.

Note that Type is now part of the identifier

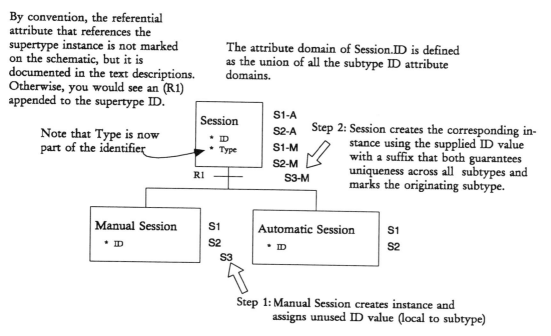

Step 2: Session creates the corresponding instance using the supplied ID value with a suffix that both guarantees uniqueness across all subtypes and marks the originating subtype.

Step 1: Manual Session creates instance and assigns unused ID value (local to subtype)

**Model 6.8**

So each subtype generates identifier values, blissfully ignorant of what any of the other subtypes are doing. But it's okay, because the Session.Type attribute domain contains a letter or name for each subtype which can be suffixed to the local identifier when it is placed in the supertype. Remember, with the percolation method the Type attribute must be a component of the supertype object identifier.

This brings us to the next question.

# Which policy should you use?

I generally try to adopt the existing application rules. But sometimes the existing rules are screwy.

**Use existing policies**

Often policies are already in place that determine how instances are labeled. If you are building a supertype relationship that distinguishes two types of stereo cables; RCA and 1/4 inch and there is already a convention in place where cables are named R1, R2, R3 and Q1, Q2, Q3 then it is probably easiest to use the percolation strategy.

**Impose a labeling scheme**

On the other hand, if there is no policy in place, or if the existing policy is flawed so that ambiguous labels could potentially be generated, then it is your responsibility as the analyst to impose a good labeling scheme.[1]

Now you have to make a guess about the state models that will manipulate the supertype relationship objects. If you are going to put all or most of the processing in the supertype, then the trickle down strategy makes more sense. If you know that you will build a separate state model for each subtype, then the percolation strategy may be the best idea.

If you don't know - then don't worry. Just pick one of the policies. If you make a bad decision, you will know it when you start building the state models, and the change to the information model will be minor.

---

[1] Which, after all, is a lot more fun.

# Frequently asked questions about supertype relationships

**When should an object be subtyped according to its states?**

Normally, the states of an object appear in a state model, not the information model. But sometimes you need to create a separate subtype object for each state or primary state in the supertype object's state model. Model 6.3 is a perfect example. You should do this only when

- one or more relationships make sense in some states but not in others, or

- one or more attributes make sense in some states but not in others.

*Chapter 7*

# Advanced supertype relationships

We reviewed the plain vanilla supertype relationship in the last chapter:

But there are even more powerful things you can do with supertypes that look like this:

**Multidirectional supertyping**      **Multilevel supertyping**      **Overlapping supertypes**

Let's examine what these constructs mean and study some examples where they are useful as well as not so useful.

## Multidirectional supertyping

First let's jump right into an example application.

APPLICATION NOTE

In a submarine computer game we need to model how torpedoes are carried and deployed on virtual submarines. A limited number of torpedoes is initially loaded onto a submarine. These torpedoes are stored safely in racks until they are needed for battle. When ordered by the captain, a torpedo may be loaded into an empty torpedo tube. The tube is flooded and then, when the order is given, the torpedo is fired. At this point, the torpedo is ejected from the tube and the torpedo swims under its own power toward a designated target.

The torpedo lifecycle is illustrated below:

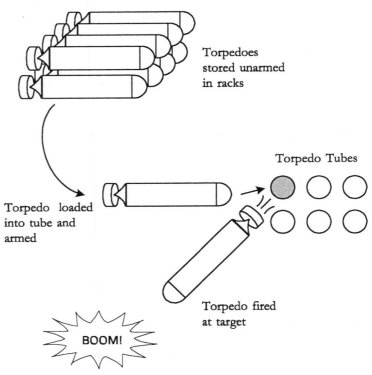

**Figure 7.1**

Notice that the relationship between a torpedo and a tube is only meaningful when a torpedo is in its LOADED state. It stands to reason that there might be attributes that are meaningful only in certain torpedo states. Consequently, it is a good idea to subtype torpedo according to its primary modes of operation.

Here's a first cut at a model.

**Model 7.1**

Now let's complicate matters...

APPLICATION NOTE

Two torpedo designs are used aboard submarines in this game.

The first type of torpedo is guided by a virtual wire that is reeled out of the back of the torpedo as it swims toward its target. Commands and data are sent back and forth along this wire until the spool runs out. At this point the wire is cut. If the torpedo has not found its target by then, it commences a descending spiral search pattern until it either hits something or runs out of fuel. Often the torpedo will be detonated just prior to running out of wire to minimize the risk of having the torpedo hit the sub from which it originated.

The other type of torpedo is smart. It has no wire and is entirely self-guided. As the torpedo is loaded, a search program is selected and target parameters are downloaded into the torpedo.

117

If it weren't for the subtyping of Torpedo in Model 7.1, we would be able to draw this alternate model:

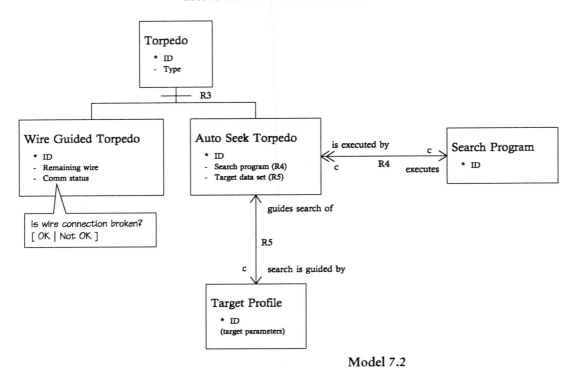

**Model 7.2**

This model subtypes Torpedo according to guidance procedure. We have accounted for the amount of remaining wire and whether the wire is broken. Auto Seek Torpedoes are more complex. It will take more than a couple of attributes to define the guidance heuristics. Relationship R4 models the selection of a Search Program that guides an Auto Seek Torpedo. The content of the Search Program is the subject of another subsystem or problem domain. R4 is conditional on the many side since a single program is fairly standard and may be in use by any number of Auto Seek Torpedoes, including zero at any given moment. A Target Profile is more specific, however. Each Target Profile is created specifically for a given Auto Seek Torpedo. The details of the Target Profile are also beyond the scope of this example.

This subtyping works fine, but how do we account for the application facts originally captured in Model 7.1?

We would like to combine Model 7.1 and Model 7.2 to get the following model which simultaneously subtypes in two directions:

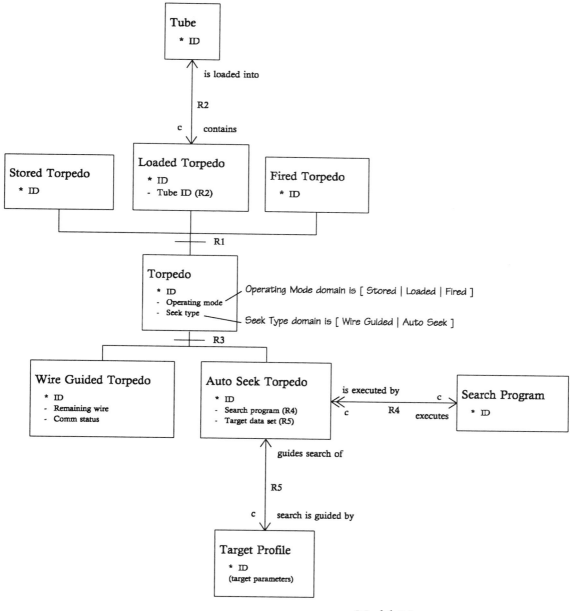

Model 7.3

**Is multidirectional subtyping legal?**

Can we get away with this? In other words,

- Is this kind of two-way subtyping legal?

- If so, does the model say what we want it to?

As always, when we aren't sure about model syntax, we have to examine the underlying instances and table rules. We know that a normal supertype relationship formalizes the partitioning of a set (see "Set partitioning" on page 96). A two-way subtyping as shown in Model 7.3 completely partitions the same set of example instances two independent ways as shown below:

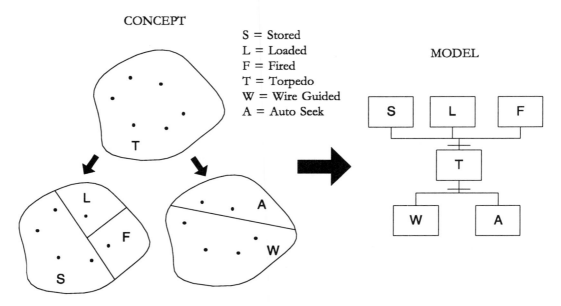

CONCEPT

S = Stored
L = Loaded
F = Fired
T = Torpedo
W = Wire Guided
A = Auto Seek

MODEL

**Figure 7.2**

Notice that every instance has exactly three set memberships: (T), (A or W) and (S, L or F).

It is easy enough to draw a set that is partitioned more than one way, so we ought to be able to subtype an object more than one way. We have to be careful, however, not to end up generating duplicate identifiers and ensure that the appropriate referential attributes are in place. In other words, we must obey the fundamental table rules set forth in Chapters 1 and 2.

**Multidirectional subtype identifier schemes**

Let's see how each of the identifier strategies (percolation and trickle down), described for supertype relationships in Chapter 6, applies to a two-way subtype.

**Trickle down - multidirectional**

This is probably the easiest approach and it is the one I chose for Model 7.3. You can imagine that if all instances originate in the supertype object, Torpedo, you won't have to worry about duplicate IDs. You just assign identifier values T1, T2, T3, ... , in the Torpedo object and let the ID value trickle down into the subtypes by reference. Wire Guided Torpedo.ID, for example, would be a referential attribute referring to Torpedo.ID.

Here are some instances that trickle down:

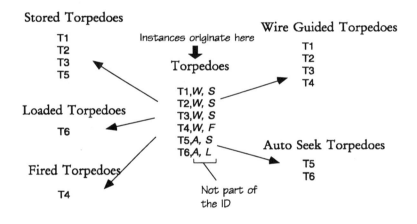

**Figure 7.3**

As you can see, the trickle down method does a fine job of keeping IDs unique across all objects in a multidirectional supertype relationship.

**Percolate up - multidirectional**

We could instead create the instances and assign identifiers in the subtype objects. But which ones? It would make the most sense to create instances in the Wire Guided/Auto Seek subtypes. This is because instances do not migrate between these two subtypes. Once an instance is created as a Wire Guided Torpedo, it is always a Wire Guided Torpedo.

Here are some instances that percolate up from the right side into the supertype object and then trickle down to subtypes on the left:

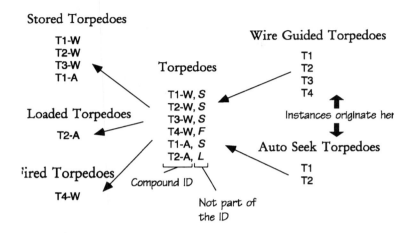

**Figure 7.4**

This also works, but we need to modify Model 7.3 accordingly.

Model 7.3 can be adjusted to support the percolate up scheme as shown below:

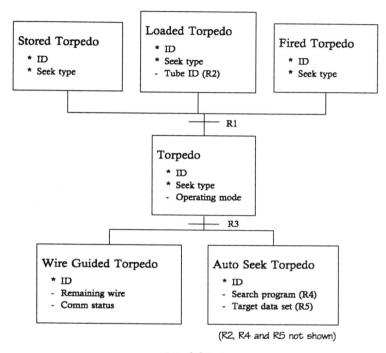

Model 7.4

The attribute Torpedo.Seek Type is necessary since the Wire Guided and Auto Seek subtypes are generating identifiers independently. This compound identifier must be carried into each of the operating mode subtypes. The type attribute resolves duplication in the situation, for example, when a Wire Guided Torpedo T2 and an Auto Seek Torpedo T2 are both in storage.

So we've dealt with the question of whether two-way subtyping is syntactically correct. Yes, you can do it. But, as we shall see, this is usually a bad idea.

**Why multidirectional subtyping is usually a bad idea**

The crux of the problem lies in this principle of the multidirectional subtype construct:

> Each subtyping on the supertype object is totally independent of the other subtyping.

123

You can be sure that sooner or later a previously overlooked or newly introduced requirement will arise that negates this independence. In fact, it's going to happen in our submarine application. Consider the following overlooked requirements:

1.  Relationships R4 and R5 are conditional because they don't apply when an Auto Seek Torpedo is in storage.

2.  A number of Wire Guided attributes need to be added, such as Desired Heading, Desired Speed, Actual Heading and Actual Speed, which apply only when a Wire Guided Torpedo is Fired.

The two subtype directions are no longer independent. The Desired Heading attribute is relevant only to Wire Guided Torpedoes (An Auto Seek Torpedo determines its own heading). We are tempted to place Desired Heading in the Wire Guided Torpedo object, but then our model would say that all Wire Guided Torpedoes have a desired heading. But only a Wire Guided Torpedo that has been Fired can be commanded. We can't place Desired Heading in the Fired Torpedo subtype because then it would apply to both Fired and Auto Seek Torpedoes, which is not what we want.

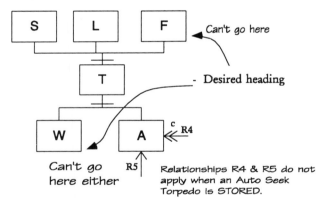

**Figure 7.5**

Furthermore, relationships R4 and R5 can be made unconditional but only for Auto Seek Torpedoes that are either Loaded or Fired, but not Stored.

The two-way subtype forced us into a modeling corner that we can escape only by totally abandoning the multidirectional supertype approach. Instead, we can supertype in multiple levels.

# Multilevel supertyping

Everything that we wanted to model with a multidirectional subtype can be accomplished using multiple levels instead. Here the torpedo model is recast as a multilevel supertype:

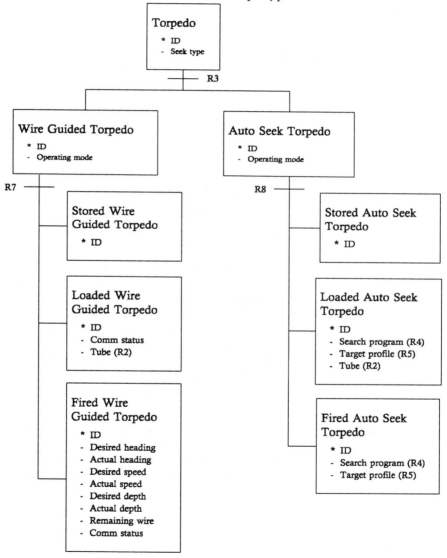

Model 7.5

Let's go back and look at sets of instances. The multidirectional and multilevel subset partition schemes are compared below:

Multidirectional partitioning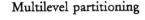Multilevel partitioning

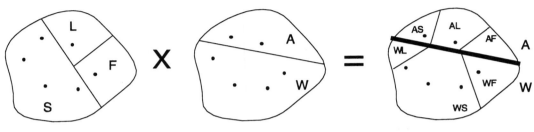

**Figure 7.6**

With multilevel partitioning the set of Torpedoes is first partitioned into Auto Seek and Wire Guided Torpedoes. Then each of these subsets is further partitioned into Stored, Loaded and Fired Torpedoes. You can see that we don't lose anything in the translation. In fact, we pick up a few sets that we didn't have before.

**Better precision**

The advantage of this approach is that we can be much more specific about torpedo capabilities. With the multidirectional Model 7.4, we could make statements about a Torpedo of a particular type OR a Torpedo in a particular operating mode. The multilevel Model 7.5, on the other hand, can make statements about a particular type of Torpedo in a specific situation. For example, Model 7.5 says that a Fired Wire Guided Torpedo has some special command parameters (Desired Heading, Speed, etc.) that are not relevant to any other torpedo type in any other mode of operation.

**Better adaptation to future requirements**

Of course, not all the subtypes have special characteristics. A Stored Wire Guided Torpedo has no special attributes or relationships. Will any develop in the future? Well, that's just the point. Any newly discovered attributes or relationships are more likely to have a place to go. Model 7.5 will adapt more easily to new requirements than Model 7.4.

**Questions that probe deeper**

More importantly, Model 7.5 forces us to ask probing questions about the application that are more likely to be overlooked with Model 7.4. Are Stored Wire Guided Torpedoes organized the same as Stored Auto Seek Torpedoes? Can you send any commands to an Auto Seek

Torpedo once it is fired? Can you download any parameters in advance into a Loaded Wire Guided Torpedo?

# Overlapping supertypes (selective generalization)

In all the fuss over torpedo specialization, we created some loose ends. What happened to relationships R4 and R5 from Model 7.3? And whatever happened to R2? Thanks to the new objects added in Model 7.5, there is now more than one place for each of these relationships to connect up. This can be fixed by generalizing.

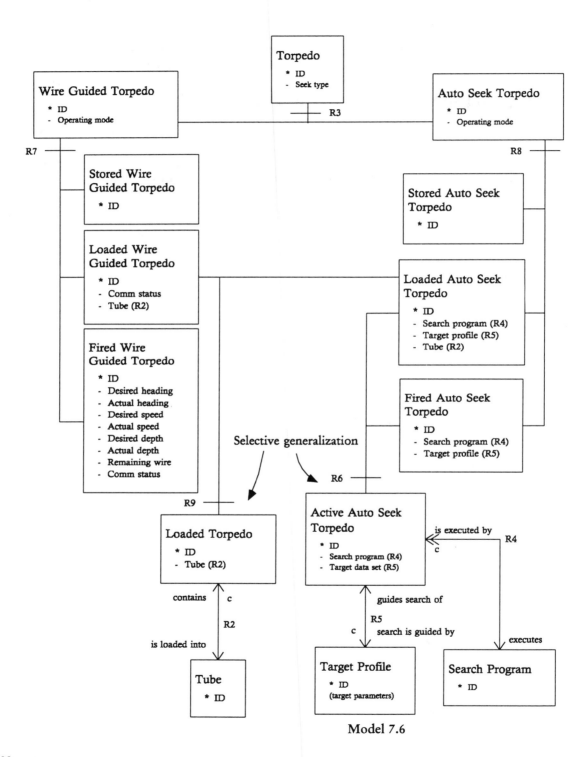

Model 7.6

Two new supertypes have been created that join together some of the Wire Guided and Auto Seek Torpedo subtypes. The Loaded Torpedo object represents the union of all Loaded Wire Guided and Loaded Auto Seek Torpedoes. A Loaded Torpedo, by definition, must be in a Tube. Consequently, R2 is now unconditional on the Tube side.

Since relationships R4 and R5 apply to both Loaded and Fired Auto Seek Torpedoes, they are connected to the newly created Active Auto Seek Torpedo object. The supertype object definition allows us to make R4 unconditional on the Search Program side and R5 unconditional on the Target Profile side.

**Overlapping sets**    Let's see how some generic instances might be grouped:

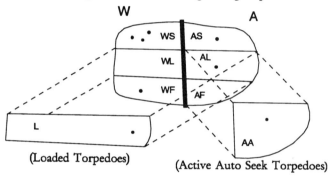

**Figure 7.7**

The two new objects, Loaded Torpedo and Active Auto Seek Torpedo, are designated as sets L and AA. Set L is the union of sets WL and AL, while set AA is the union of sets AL and AF. Note that sets L and AA overlap on AL. So membership in AL necessitates simultaneous membership in five sets: T, A, AL, L and AA. In our model, this means that an instance of Loaded Auto Seek Torpedo must always have corresponding instances in Torpedo, Auto Seek Torpedo, Loaded Torpedo and Active Auto Seek Torpedo to formalize the set memberships.

Now we have the powerful ability to break down any set into non-overlapping subsets, at multiple levels, and then to unify those subsets in any combination that we need.

Note the Operating Mode attributes in the Wire Guided and Auto Seek Torpedo objects cannot be promoted into the Torpedo supertype. Why? The names are the same, but each attribute domain is defined differently. The domain of Wire Guided Torpedo.Operation Mode is [Stored WGT, Loaded WGT, Fired WGT], while the domain of Auto Seek Torpedo.Operating Mode is [Stored AST, Loaded AST, Fired AST]. This distinction might seem silly until you decide someday that Auto Seek Torpedoes require more or less subtypes than Wire Guided Torpedoes.

The only problem is that the Comm Status attribute appears in both the Loaded and Fired Wire Guided Torpedo objects. We can take the generalization a step further to produce the following model:

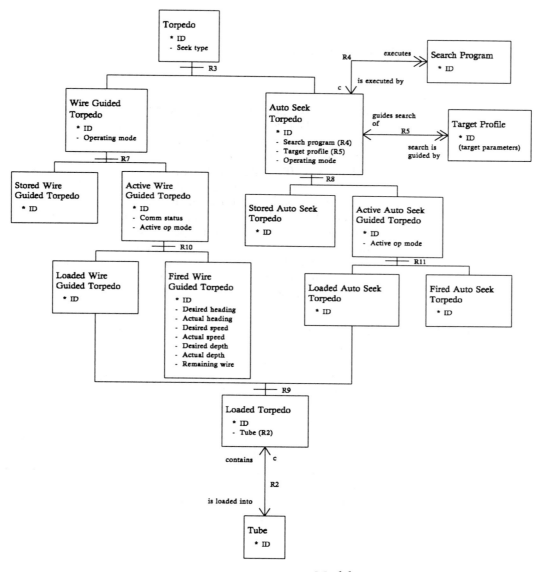

**Model 7.7**

**Eliminating duplicate attributes**

As you can see, that's quite a change just to accommodate one trouble-some attribute, leading me to the following two points: (1) No matter what the situation, you can always come up with an arrangement of supertype relationships that eliminates duplicate attributes. (2) Just because you can eliminate duplicate attributes doesn't mean you should. If the trees get in the way of the forest, you might end up hacking yourself into a corner.[1]

# The danger of supertype hacking

**Don't waste time with minute details**

It is important to do thorough analysis. If you collect attributes one by one, rearranging your subtypes each time to achieve optimal generalization, then you may be thrashing with your model forever. It's normal to sketch out a variety of relationship and object combinations, some of them quite unwieldy, before settling on a concise, yet stable result. (By stable result I mean a model that can incorporate minute requirements changes without being completely rearranged like a trailer park in a tornado). It is a common mistake to try to achieve this stability by hacking a model to death, rather than by investigating the application properly. Nonmodeling analysis activities (see see Chapter 8, on page 143."How to avoid model hacking" on page 143) may lead to some insight about the application that would do more to simplify your work in a few minutes than another week of object juggling.

**How to avoid thrashing**

For example, let's say that Model 7.6 generated a lot of questions about torpedoes. I wouldn't waste another minute trying to produce Model 7.7 just to get the Comm Status attribute into the same object. Instead, I would first get my questions answered. I would conduct interviews, draw informal diagrams to confirm my understanding, and search every scrap of documentation and requirements relating to torpedo features that I could find. Only then would I go back and try recasting my model. By then the Comm Status attribute might have become a moot point. Maybe there was yet another type of torpedo - not in use, but planned, that had not been considered. Maybe I would have discovered other attributes or concepts that would lead to a very different model. Then, again, maybe I wouldn't find anything new. In that case, I would go ahead and produce Model 7.7. Let your understanding of the application fuel the model tweaking and not the other way around.

---

[1]Or worse yet, mixing metaphors.

# How to organize subtype levels

Going back to Model 7.6, let's consider a question that hasn't been addressed yet. We subtyped Torpedo into Wire Guided/Auto Seek and then into Stored/Loaded/Fired. But couldn't we have done it the other way around? Why not first subtype Torpedo into Stored/Loaded/Fired and then subtype each of these objects into Auto Seek and Wire Guided?

From a table/set/information model perspective, there isn't much difference between the two approaches. But if you move along to the state models, there is a big difference that favors the approach used in Model 7.6.

# Subtype migration

Subtype instance behavior can be classified in these ways:

- Migrating subtypes
- Nonmigrating subtypes

**Migrating subtypes**  Both ways of subtyping are employed in our torpedo example. Consider the Wire Guided Torpedo:

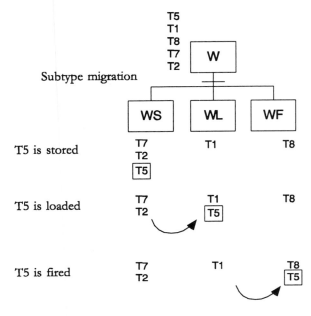

**Figure 7.8**

An instance of Wire Guided Torpedo starts out with a corresponding instance of Stored Wire Guided Torpedo (WS). When the Torpedo is loaded into a tube, the instance of Wire Guided Torpedo stays in place, but its corresponding instance in WS moves to Loaded (WL). In other words, the WS instance is deleted and a new corresponding instance is created in WL. Eventually, the WL instance hops over to Fired (WF). This is what is meant by subtype migration.

**Nonmigrating subtypes**   Now contrast this subtype behavior with a nonmigrating subtype on Torpedo:

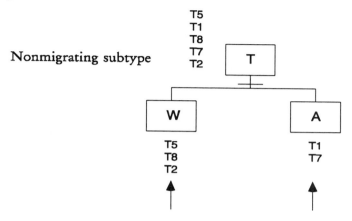

Figure 7.9

When a Torpedo is created it is either an Auto Seek or a Wire Guided Torpedo. End of story. One cannot be converted into the other - in this application anyway.

Now let's take a look at all the migration that occurs with each arrangement of subtype levels:

Easy migration

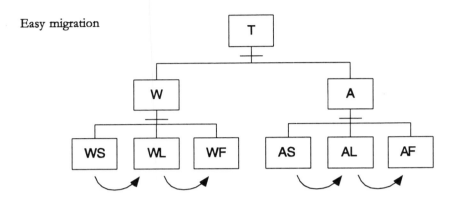

Awkward migration

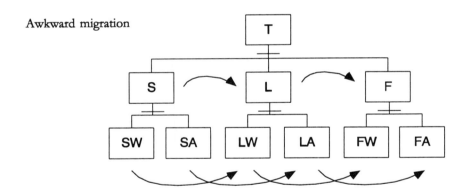

**Figure 7.10**

As you can see, we won't have to create and delete so many instances if we go with the first approach. It is a good idea to subtype in such a way that you simplify dynamic behavior.

## When to subtype an object according to its states

In the Torpedo models introduced in this chapter, we subtyped a Torpedo for two different reasons. The Wire Guided/Auto Seek subtyping allowed for different Torpedo guidance behavior. The Stored/ Loaded/Fired subtyping accounted for different Torpedo operating modes. The Wire Guided/Auto Seek subtyping seemed to jump right out of the application description. But what about the Stored/Loaded/Fired subtyping? The need wasn't so obvious.

**Look for states where relationships and attribute relevance changes**

The behavior of every object in an information model can be characterized by a state model. But we don't subtype every object according to its states. So why did we subtype Wire Guided and Auto Seek Torpedoes according to their STORED-LOADED-FIRED states? We did it because there were relationships and attributes that were relevant only in certain states. In fact, the state model for a Wire Guided Torpedo probably has more than just the STORED-LOADED-FIRED states. Other states might be INITIALIZING-ARMING-RESETTING. In fact, the state model for Wire Guided Torpedo must either move the subtype instance, or generate events that result in the migration of the corresponding subtype instance in the STORED-LOADED-FIRED states.

## Don't overdo the hierarchical thing

If you end up with a supertype relationship with many levels, like this one...

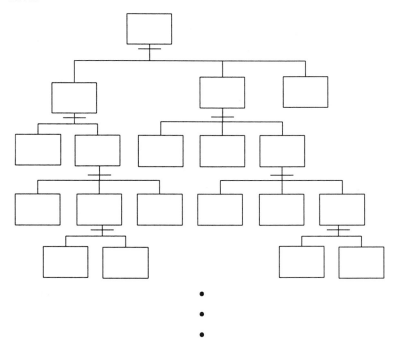

...then you are probably doing something terribly wrong. A structure like this is inherently unstable. The deeper the hierarchy, the more likely there is an attribute or relationship somewhere that breaks the hierarchical paradigm. Odd combinations of attributes and objects conspire to subvert the hierarchy and complicate the state models.

If you are presented with a suspiciously hierarchical model like the one here, look for common behavior, attributes or relationships in the subtype extremities that aren't properly generalized in a single supertype. For example, you might find an attribute with the same name throughout subtypes on the leftmost and rightmost sides of the tree. This will lead you to join some of the subtypes into supertype objects, thus creating more of a layered structure.

## Sometimes the wrong thing is subtyped

You can get into a lot of trouble when you subtype the wrong object.

APPLICATION NOTE

Let's say, for example that we are building a system that tracks defective braces. The brace may be defective because it is bent, sheared or cracked. When it is bent, it has a bend angle. When it is cracked, we are concerned about the crack depth.

Here is a first stab at a model of brace defects:

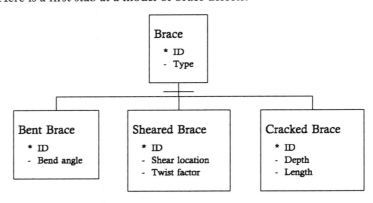

**Model 7.8**

This model says that

a Brace may be a Bent Brace, a Sheared Brace, or a Cracked Brace.

But what if a Brace is both sheared and cracked? You can't create two instances in the Brace object with each defect because one Brace is one Brace - not two!

And what instance do you create when you have a Brace that is not defective? Let's review the application rules:

- If a Brace is normal, it is not sheared, bent, or cracked.

- A Brace may be bent, sheared, cracked, or some combination.

Since a Brace is either normal or defective, this idea could be subtyped. But defects don't necessarily exclude each other - so a subtype doesn't seem appropriate.

The key is in the use of the word "defect". A Brace can be normal, or it might have some combination of defects, which leads us to this model:

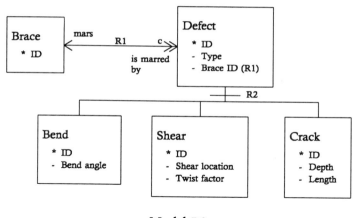

**Model 7.9**

This model says that a Brace has zero, one or many Defects. A Defect may be a Bend, Shear, or a Crack.

So with Model 7.9 we handle the case when a Brace is normal. A normal Brace has no Defects. That's why R1 is conditional. In addition, this model allows a Brace to have any combination of Defects. In fact, this model states that a Brace can have more than one Defect of the same type.

# Summary

In this chapter we have examined the multidirectional, multilevel and overlapping supertype patterns. These patterns are summarized as follows:

**Multidirectional supertyping** - An object participates as a supertype in more than one supertype relationship. Each supertype relationship is subtyped using completely independent criteria.

**Multilevel supertyping** - An object is subtyped according to one criterion; then some or all of the subtypes are further subtyped.

**Overlapping supertypes** - Some subtype objects from one or more different supertype relationships are brought together to form another supertype.

These patterns make it possible to model general rules about an object while also exposing varying levels of exceptions and local degrees of commonality.

# How to build useful models 2

# Chapter 8

# How to avoid model hacking

The formal nature of Shlaer-Mellor OOA is no guard against developing bad modeling habits. As with any skill, bad habits are easily acquired, impede your progress and are difficult to throw off. I would like to warn you about the worst of these... model hacking.

We are all familiar with the code hacking syndrome. That's where you root around in a mass of code that doesn't quite work. Rather than step back and rethink the underlying design, it is tempting to make just one more minor adjustment to the code, recompile and then see what happens. If it doesn't work, then you repeat the cycle repeatedly until the code seems to work. We all hack, but as experienced programmers we know how dangerous and unproductive this process can be. Hacking yields quick and dirty fixes. It does not lead to sophisticated systems that are reliable, extendable, or maintainable.

In fact, that's why we do ANALYSIS. Question: Now that we are building models, are we immune to the hacking syndrome? Not a chance! It's just as easy to get mired in a tar pit of ugly models as it is to get whipped up into an endless code hacking frenzy.

Let's take a look at how model hacking occurs, review its symptoms and then see how hacking can be avoided - or at least minimized.

Model hacking is exactly the same as code hacking without the benefit of a compiler.[1] When you are introduced to the tools provided by a modeling language, it's natural to want to immediately apply them to some problem. The next thing you know, you're sketching rectangles and arrows like crazy. You reflect on those estimates you heard in class about analysts producing an average of one object per day - sometimes less. Obviously, that must apply to people less intelligent and industrious, because you have just drawn dozens of objects in under an hour.

**The symptoms of model hacking**

Unfortunately, you are headed for trouble. Sooner or later one or more of the following problems arise:

- You can't tell if your model is capturing the rules you set out to formalize.

- You have a hard time convincing anyone that your model is correct and appropriate to the problem at hand.

- Past some number of objects (4? 7? 10?) additional objects and relationships add annoying redundancies and inconsistencies to your initially pristine model.

- You find it excruciatingly difficult to model some concept that should be simple and intuitive.

- People nod politely when you explain your model, but you can tell that they don't really get it.

- (consequently) You get no useful feedback on your work.

---

[1] Advances in model translation technology are rapidly eroding this distinction.

- You dutifully model rules given to you by application experts only to find out later that the "experts" were wrong.[1]

- You have no idea whether your model is complete - or ever will be.

So what's causing all this trouble? Is it a deficiency in the Shlaer-Mellor method? - No. Operator error? - Yes! All the problems listed are classic symptoms of model hacking. Too much effort has been expended on building and revising models while essential analysis activities are being ignored.

**The difference between modeling and analysis**

That's the real problem. It is easy to confuse modeling with analysis. It took me years to appreciate the critical distinction between these two activities. Modeling is the process of formalizing an idea using elements of a language. Analysis, on the other hand, encompasses many tasks:

- Finding, collecting and organizing data (very unglamorous)

- Brainstorming

- Presenting and reviewing alternative concepts (not necessarily models)

- Sketching out informal ideas on the white-board (or cocktail napkins)

- Generalizing, simplifying, abstracting

- Arguing

- Skillful interviewing (the expert system people have some interesting methods)

- Taking and publishing good technical notes

And, oh yes...

- Modeling

**Focus on the analysis**

The frustrations I listed earlier do not result so much from bad modeling skill as they do from inadequately performing the nonmodeling analysis tasks. Unfortunately, the schedule pressure to produce a complete model of 30 objects in four weeks causes panic. This panic results in 80% of your time hunched over an information model that will never be any good. Spend 60%-80% on the nonmodeling analysis

---

[1]Wrong = incomplete, oversimplified, half-baked - to name a few.

tasks in the previous list, and you will produce a more clear, concise and useful information model.

Productive Analysis Time Allocation

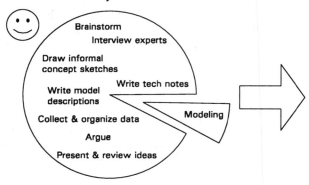

Steady progress, solid models, close match to application requirements, models build upon one another nicely

Time invested in analysis pays off

Material can be interpreted and used by those not well versed in the modeling language

Unproductive Analysis Time Allocation

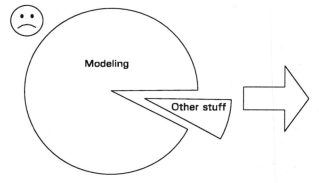

Lot's of models generated quickly

Models never validated, difficult to integrate models and most of the work never reaches implementation

Analysis paralysis inevitable

Nothing generated of value to those not well versed in modeling language

Figure 8.1

**Draw informal sketches**   The best way to focus the nonmodeling analysis tasks is to produce what I call "informal sketches". Let's see how this works using an application example.

APPLICATION NOTE

We have a set of robots, lights, and roller coaster conveyors in a Disneyland-like theme park that we want to control. Different sets of controls are available for each of these things. Lights have intensity, on/off status, color, filter type, and 3-D position. The track car has a 1-D position and a speed. During a show, each of these controllable objects can have its characteristics changed in a preprogrammed way. To program a light, for example, the desired 3-D position, intensity, and filter at a handful of intermediate points are specified. If t is time, at t=0 the light will be at a certain x,y,z with an intensity i and a filter level f. At t=2.4 it will have different values for some or all of x,y,z,i, and t. Using a smooth interpolation algorithm, the values between the times t=0 and t=2.4 will be computed and used for control while the show is running. On the other hand, the light might not be used at all and remain stationary and powered down for the entire show.

We want a way to program the intermediate values for all the controllable objects so that they can later be driven in realtime.

Before getting to the informal sketches (don't look at Figure 8.2 yet), imagine that the information model in Model 8.1 has been presented to you as a solution and that you are (pick one):

a)   the manager

b)   an application expert

c)   the analyst (returning to your model after four weeks in the Caribbean)

## Formal Model

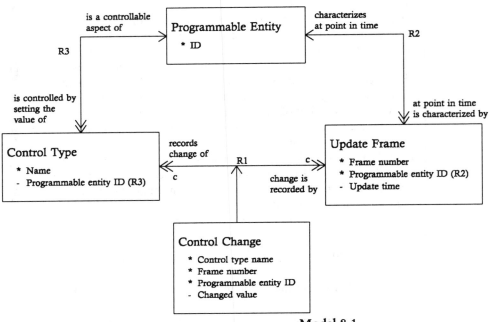

**Model 8.1**

Does Model 8.1 compare different approaches to representing control changes? Does it show you how the scenario in the problem description might work? What does the model say? Let's see, a Programmable Entity is controlled by setting the value of one or more Control Types. A Programmable Entity at a point in time is characterized by one or more Update Frames. (Yawn) You can tell that the model is syntactically correct, but is it the right model?

My point is this: It doesn't matter how much information modeling experience you have; when you are presented with a new model, you don't see the application. All you see are boxes, arrows and names that you don't understand. Especially if the model is large, complex and, ugh... poorly laid out.

Now look at the informal sketch I have drawn in Figure 8.2.

## Application Domain Objects

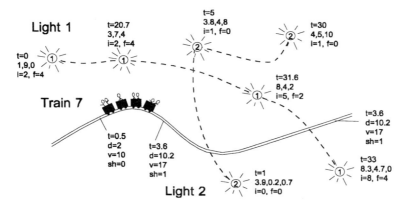

## Animation Domain Objects

### Programmable Entities

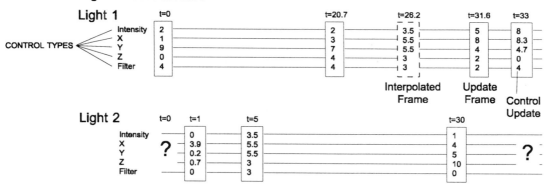

**Figure 8.2**

It might seem a bit cryptic, but doesn't it look a lot more like the application description than all those boxes and arrows in Model 8.1?

**Formal models versus informal sketches**

Let's compare the two approaches.

An information model

- is an abstraction of all cases, not just the one you think about most of the time,

- can be integrated with other modeled concepts, all using a uniform language,

- yields an unambiguous interpretation,

- can be mapped directly to an implementation,

- forces specific policy decisions and

- imposes a vocabulary on the problem.

Whereas an informal sketch

- lets you use whatever symbols you like,

- can be read and understood quickly by anyone familiar with the application,

- is less work to produce than a model, so you can compare and discard approaches more economically,

- describes a problem in terms of real examples rather than abstractions, thus keeping you in touch with reality and

- is not necessarily object-oriented.

I draw informal sketches prior to modeling as I collect and verify facts about the application. Then I model what I have sketched. When I get bogged down in modeling confusion, I go back to sketching. If I can't sketch a problem, then I either need more data or I need more coffee.

In order of importance, I draw informal sketches to:

**Think:** You can't model what you can't sketch.

**Collect Information:** A good sketch elicits better feedback from more people than does a bunch of obscure rectangles and arrows.

**Communicate and Verify:** Your illustrated technical notes will keep colleagues informed and off your back while they wait for your completed models.

**Document:** We all know the value of documentation. By the way, you can paste some of your sketches into the object descriptions. Notice that I listed documentation fourth in importance.

The process of informal sketching helps you to focus on the critical nonmodeling analysis tasks, which will aid you immeasurably in producing good models. Not only that - it's much more fun than model hacking.

The entire analysis process is summarized (and admittedly oversimplified) as a flow chart on the next page.

# How to build an object model

Start

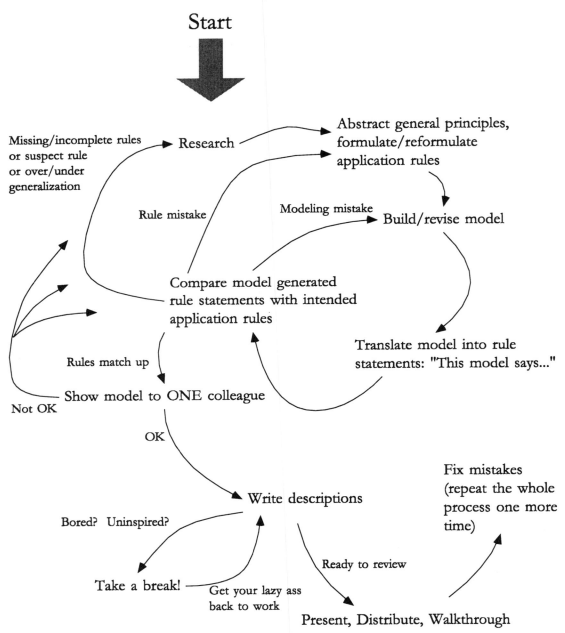

Missing/incomplete rules
or suspect rule
or over/under
generalization

Research

Abstract general principles,
formulate/reformulate
application rules

Rule mistake

Modeling mistake

Build/revise model

Compare model generated
rule statements with intended
application rules

Translate model into rule
statements: "This model says..."

Rules match up

Show model to ONE colleague

Not OK

OK

Write descriptions

Fix mistakes
(repeat the whole
process one more
time)

Bored? Uninspired?

Take a break!

Get your lazy ass
back to work

Ready to review

Present, Distribute, Walkthrough

# Chapter 9          Why write model descriptions?

When you look at a network of objects and relationships laid out on a sheet of paper, don't fool yourself into thinking that you are looking at a complete information model. That would be like mistaking an outline for a whole book. What you are really looking at is just an easy-reference graphic summary of an information model. The real work is in the text and drawings that constitute the model descriptions.

I don't know how many times I've been handed an information model with skimpy or nonexistent descriptions. As an experienced modeler I can verify the model syntax (Are all the referential attributes in the right place? Is this associative object formalized correctly?). And the syntax is generally in good shape. But modeling skill won't tell me what each of the objects, attributes and relationships mean. The authors of the model must explain their work to me verbally. As soon as the explanation starts, the authors invariably become aware of missing attributes, incorrect relationships and all manner of ambiguity, uncertainty and handwaving.

It's this process of explanation that forces a closer examination of what the authors previously considered to be pretty much complete. What I find interesting is that this scenario plays itself out only when the descriptions are deficient. Whenever I am handed a model with complete descriptions, most of the errors in the model tend to be minor syntax issues. But even the most subtle application requirements are well addressed.

The ant says it best.

> **If you want to build useful information models, write those !#$!! descriptions!**

**How do you write good descriptions?** The following three chapters provide detailed guidelines for writing object, attribute and relationship descriptions that yield useful information models. If you like building things, but hate writing - like me - then you are probably still wondering why the descriptions are worth all the bother.

When I started building information models, I didn't pay much attention to the model descriptions. But as I developed more and more models on more and more projects, I experienced many ugly setbacks that hampered productivity and resulted in wasted time. Many of these setbacks could be traced to flawed model descriptions.

The only real way to learn how to write good descriptions is to experience the consequences of not writing them! You need to know precisely why you are writing the descriptions and how you are going to use them later on. Unfortunately, this experience takes time to accumulate. Hopefully, the advice in the next few chapters will reduce the amount of experience you need to acquire to produce effective information models.

## Five reasons to write model descriptions

The following reasons are ranked in order of importance from the perspective of the analyst, not the model reviewer.

### ① INCREASE THE QUALITY OF YOUR MODEL

Documentation is not the primary reason for writing model descriptions. If it was, I would get to them sometime after I organized that junk drawer under my kitchen phone.

The most important reason for writing model descriptions is to improve the technical quality of the concepts you are modeling. True, that is the same reason for writing technical notes. But technical notes and model descriptions contribute to the quality of a model in different ways.

**The goals of technical notes and model descriptions are different**

A technical note may collect information, propose or compare concepts, and explore scenarios. But when you produce a model description, you are taking a stand on a single approach that you define in detail. It is okay for a technical note to be full of loose ends. The model descriptions, on the other hand, must demonstrate that the model is internally consistent.

The informal technical notes generate the raw concepts which are refined to produce the formal model descriptions. Yet I always end up copying or referencing subsets of the technical note text and diagrams in the model descriptions.

**Don't get cocky**

As you develop experience building information models, it is easy to get cocky. I don't know how many times I have had discussions, written technical notes, and sketched out a model that I characterized as "being pretty much complete" - except for a little documentation. I always find it hard to believe that I am going to learn anything substantially new by writing a bunch of descriptions. All manner of rationalizations bounce around in my head, like "Sure, I always nag other engineers to write complete descriptions, but I've been modeling for years. This model is based on principles learned from an earlier project. I know what I am doing and I have this subsystem all figured out. Oh, well - I'll just get this little documentation task out of the way..."

But there is something about the process of writing model descriptions that makes you consider subtle policies and boundary conditions that you missed in the technical notes. With a 25-object model, I end up discovering at least five to ten holes in my thinking. By "holes" I mean cases I didn't consider, questions I didn't ask, policies that need to be established, and behavior that wasn't obvious.

The activity of model description is a crucial thinking process. If you want to produce useful, well thought out models, you have to write good descriptions.

## ② MAGNIFY YOUR EXPERTISE (AVOID LOOKING STUPID)

It's easy to become an authority when you write good model descriptions. The creation of information model descriptions is the analysis equivalent of writing code (well, the data structure code anyway). Watch what happens after you wallow around in the details of your model for a while. When you are in a conference and someone brings up one of the issues relevant to your subsystem you will suddenly find yourself answering questions and resolving issues with a precise vocabulary and an extremely clear understanding of the problem that will amaze, if not intimidate, your colleagues.

Of course, anyone can read your descriptions and approach your level of expertise. Your goal is to share rather than monopolize information. But you always develop more intimacy with subsystems you write about than with those that you merely review.

## ③ AVOID HAVING THE SAME ARGUMENT OVER AND OVER AND OVER...

My team was plagued with a series of déjà vu experiences on an early project. There was this technical issue that took a lot of effort and argument to resolve. We thought we had killed the issue, but it kept coming back to life like the cyborg in that Terminator movie. Not only did we end up revisiting the issue every couple of months, but we kept arriving at the same conclusion! Had I written relevant object and relationship descriptions more thoroughly, I am convinced that we could have avoided this situation. To appreciate how this happened I will have to fill you in on the application a little.

**The video effects application**

We were building a system that allowed a postproduction video engineer to create a special type of animation called an effect. An effect consisted of animated entities, each of which was characterized by one or more independently editable parameters. One type of entity was a light source with four parameters: intensity and x, y, z location.

Here is a diagram of how different values could be assigned to these parameters over the course of a 3-second effect.

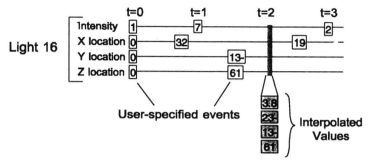

**Figure 9.1**

Each parameter had its own time line containing some number of events. When the operator pressed the RUN key, the effect would start playing at t=0 and run until the end, 3 seconds later in this case. As time progressed, every parameter would be assigned a new value. This was important because the hardware that implemented the light source needed to be fed a new set of legal values every 1/60 second.

If the current time happened to coincide with the time of an event, the parameter would assume the specified value. At t=2.5, for example, the value 19 would be assigned to the X Location attribute. When the current time was between events, some type of interpolation would occur. At t=2, Intensity would take on some value between 7 and 2 (3.8 in this case).

**The issue that wouldn't die**  So that's the background -- here's the issue. To satisfy the hardware requirement, it was argued (argument 1) that a parameter time line should contain a default event at t=0 and t=end of effect. (Every parameter is assumed to have a default value.) The user would not be allowed to delete the terminal events. In this way we could ensure that the hardware would be fed a legal control value for a parameter at all times during an effect.

**Argument 1**

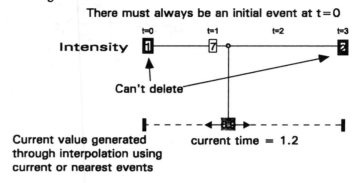

**Figure 9.2**

But the counterargument (argument 2) was that this rule placed an inconvenient restriction on the user. The user should be allowed to create or delete any events he or she wanted. It was argued that the two-event rule established a scenario analogous to the rule that prevents a user from deleting the first paragraph of a document in a word-processing application. (Naturally, the counter-counterargument was that most word processors prevent you from deleting the first page, something users don't seem to complain about.)

Argument 2 proposed that we simply feed the hardware the default parameter values whenever the running effect time did not lie between two events.

### Argument 2

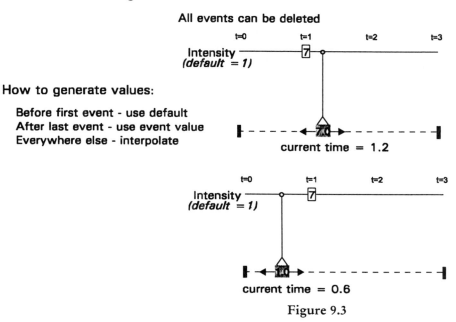

**All events can be deleted**

**How to generate values:**

Before first event - use default
After last event - use event value
Everywhere else - interpolate

Figure 9.3

But a more fundamental fact killed argument 1. We were building a second generation product. It was important to ensure that the new product would have the same animation behavior as the first-generation product. Some of the interpolation methods would generate different intermediate values over the length of a parameter time line depending on whether there were terminal events.

**A decision was made**
Each argument had its pluses and minuses. Either rule would have worked. But we had to make a decision, so we went with argument 2 primarily because reverse compatibility and simplified event editing were such compelling issues. We decided that the slightly increased complexity of the parameter value generation would not slow us down significantly.

But none of these reasons or an analysis of the competing arguments made their way into the model descriptions. In our rush to complete the models, we didn't take the time to document the reasoning behind our decision. The issue was decided and we moved on! How many similarly complex issues are handled in this manner on your project?

**How the issue resurfaced**

Over a period of 12 months spanning analysis and design, several people who weren't involved in the early decision joined the project. We had the event rule discussion with the new analyst. We had it with the user interface guy. We had it with the second user interface guy (who rethought all the policies established by the first user interface guy). We had it with one of the designers. Each time we could only remember some, but not all of the reasons for choosing our event editing approach. We remembered only that we had chosen an approach after much careful thought. We wanted new people to just accept our position without questioning it. Unfortunately, intelligent people always question assumptions. Each time the issue came up, I would try to find documentation of our first discussion. The following object description was the best I could find:

---

Excerpt from the object description of Parameter Time Line:

A Parameter Time Line is a function of time that determines values for Event-controlled Parameters. Events, which are points in time with associated Control Values, are the means by which the Parameter Time Line function is defined. These points, together with the following rules define the function:

Before the first Event, the value of Parameter is the Control Value of the first Event.

After the last Event the value of the Parameter is the Control Value of the last Event.

If there are no Events on the Parameter Time Line, the value of the Parameter is

---

As you can see, this description simply states the decision we reached. It does not document the reasoning behind the decision. While it is important to answer the what questions, it pays off in the long run if you carefully answer the why questions, also.

④ COMMUNICATE WITH FELLOW ENGINEERS

Fellow analysts, application engineers, implementers, user interface designers and others need to understand your models in detail. If subtle but important aspects of your models are misunderstood by these people, you are in for lots of frustration and wasted time.

To make your models meaningful to other people you must write good model descriptions (see ants).

**Figure 9.4**

Communication through good model descriptions pays off in many ways.

**Save time**

Good descriptions minimize the time you have to spend explaining and justifying your model. This is time you should be using to develop new ideas. Of course, even the best descriptions require some explanation. But good descriptions will elevate the technical level of discussions about your work.

**Improve progress in other subsystems**

Your models may induce progress in adjacent subsystems. Details on the edges of your subsystem, like the features of a weird jigsaw puzzle piece, may guide fellow analysts toward a solution in another part of the domain.

**Get quality feedback**

One of the best ways to increase the quality of your work is to solicit feedback. When you hand your model to a reviewer, you are looking for profound insights, not spelling errors. But without good descriptions, a reviewer cannot think about a problem in enough depth to provide useful comments. A walk-through of an information model without descriptions is a waste of time.

**Control the implementation**

It is likely that someone else will end up implementing some or all of your models. This happens even if you plan to do all the work yourself. Once implementation starts, there is always more analysis to be done. If you are a good analyst, your talent will continue to be in demand. It is therefore likely that someone else may guide your models through implementation while you generate the extra needed analysis. The descriptions you wrote will save time and steer the implementer clear of misunderstandings that would otherwise eat up lots of your valuable time.

Now put yourself in the position of an implementer, who we assume is familiar with the Shlaer-Mellor method. You are given an information model by an author you know to be bright, but not infallible. As you implement, you find yourself wanting to change one of the relationships from 1:1 to 1c:1c to make your job easier. You look up the relationship description. It doesn't make much of a case for keeping the relationship unconditional. The author is out sick for two days. You decide to change the model (or at least deviate from it in the implementation). You don't realize it yet, but this change introduces potential error states in some of the behavior models. Later on you make changes to fix that problem. As more and more of the model unravels, you refer to it less and less.[1]

The moral is this: Regardless of how badly you want to be involved in the implementation phase, write your descriptions with the assumption that someone else will do the implementation. Otherwise, you will probably miss out on the satisfaction of seeing your analysis implemented properly.

⑤ COMMUNICATE WITH YOURSELF

If you are working on a problem every day, it may seem silly to document it for your own purposes. You are already intimately familiar with the problem, so why bother writing it down? It's not like you are going to come in to work tomorrow and forget what you were working on. Even if you are a little fuzzy on some details, you can surely resurrect the details after a half hour or so. So how could it be worthwhile to spend a week writing up the descriptions when you are the only person working on the project?

When you are up to your elbows building a subsystem, it is hard to imagine that you might end up putting that subsystem on the shelf for

---

[1]Unless, of course, you are using an architecture that does 100% model translation. In that case, you will simply end up perverting the original models.

a number of months. But on every project it is necessary to put work aside at some point.

You might find that the subsystem you are working on is much larger than you thought (not unlikely). You decide to focus on one aspect of that system and set the rest aside for a while. The part you decided to focus on takes longer than anticipated to complete (likely). The next thing you know, a couple of months have gone by and there you are picking up the loose ends of the remainder of your system.

**Priorities change all the time**

Maybe management changes priorities and you find yourself working on a completely different subsystem. All that work you put in to your current subsystem ends up on the shelf for 4 months.

Maybe there aren't enough analysts to complete all of the work. You finish your subsystem. You move on to the next subsystem, and then another. Your first subsystem sits on the shelf for 6 or 7 months and now it is time to implement.

The point is that there are many scenarios where you could end up putting your partially or fully complete subsystem in cold storage for a few months. When you go back to finish that subsystem or integrate it into the other subsystems or implement it, what would you rather find? If the subsystem is even remotely interesting, you will find it contains objects that appear superfluous. What's that doing here? There will be relationships that aren't there for some reason, but you can't remember why. There are attributes that have some special significance that you forgot about. Next thing you know, you are spending weeks (that you don't have) redoing, retracing and making the same mistakes that you made originally.

## Summary

Well, there you have it. Any chimpanzee can scribble out a bunch of rectangles and arrows and claim to have completed an information model. But well thought out analysis that yields

* simple yet precise solutions to complex application requirements,
* fundamental building block concepts that readily support future extensions,

- decisions that stand up to the inevitable challenges posed by newcomers to the project, and

- a robust design that stands the test of time

doesn't pop out of a four-hour-lock-yourself-in-a-room-with-a-whiteboard-and-a-coffee-machine-gee-aren't-I-bright thinking frenzy. You have to hunker down and spend a few days - ugh - writing (and drawing). It's the only way to produce results that you and everyone else on the project can build on.

The next three chapters proceed from these (hopefully) motivating principles by showing examples of how to write useful object, attribute and relationship descriptions.

# Chapter 10

# How to write object descriptions

Here are some specific guidelines for writing object descriptions.

## Describe meaning - not syntax

We've all had the experience of trying to understand a chunk of program code written by someone else. If we are lucky, the programmer interspersed his or her code with useful comments. The comments are useful when they provide clues about how major components of the program work together. Useful comments give us insight into the thinking that generated all the code.

But of course, we are rarely so fortunate. Instead, we find comments like the following:

```
GprogQZ= ++CurrX->zur; // Increments pointer and saves it
```

So much for insight. The comment educates you about the syntax of the programming language rather than the meaning of the code.

But now we've graduated to Analysis and Design. The production of models puts us on the path to superior documentation, right? Sadly, that's not the case. It is just as easy to write useless documentation for models as it is for source code.

I'll show you what I mean with the following application:

We have a device that measures surface texture by dragging a tiny sensor across the surface of a flat sample. Typical samples are devices that must have smooth surfaces, like a flat display panel, mirror or wafer. The acquired data is a profile that consists of a series of height samples.

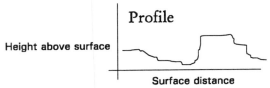

As a profile is collected, we would like to analyze the data using a variety of filters and functions. We want to make it easy to build data analysis programs for the incoming stream of data.

Using a graphical interface, an operator can access a library of data processors (functions and filters), which can be assembled into a data analysis pipeline. The output of one data processor is connected to the input of one or more data processors with a straight or branching pipe. An example pipeline is shown below:

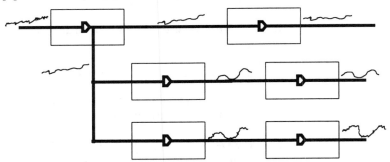

Each pipe contains data output by some data processor. The contents of each pipe may be stored or displayed.

166

Now let's take a look at part of the information model for this application.

Model 10.1

Is it completely apparent how this model formalizes the pipeline diagram? Probably not. Some objects may appear superfluous. Maybe something is missing. Without descriptions, it's hard to tell. Here are a few notes that might help: The Pipe Connection object is associative. It formalizes the relationship between two connecting Pipes (not shown). The Filter object represents an algorithm that uses certain Control Parameters to produce an output profile by taking some characteristic away (a frequency band, for example) from an incoming profile.

It isn't apparent why the Stage object is required. Why not just attach Filter directly to Pipe Connection, collapsing R11 and R13 into a single 1:M relationship? To find out more, let's consult the Stage object description.

## Stage (STG)

A Stage pumps data through a Pipe Connection. It processes data using a Filter. Note that a Filter can be applied at more than one Stage. A Stage is controlled by one or more Input Stage Parameters.

This description isn't any more helpful than the code comment at the beginning of this chapter. It doesn't say anything that isn't already obvious on the schematic. If all the descriptions are going to be like this, you would be just as well off without them.

The following description on the next page is a lot more useful.

## Stage (STG)

The term Stage refers to a stage of processing. A Stage is a place in a Pipeline where data is processed. Consider a Pipe containing data that we want to process:

Let's say that we want to reduce the noise in the signal by filtering out a band of high frequencies.

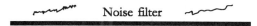

To do this we need to select a frequency filter from our library of filter functions, create a stage, split the pipe, and then insert the stage.

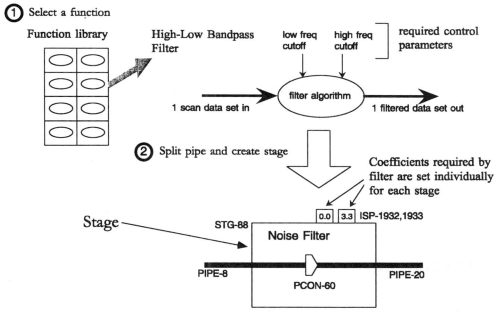

A Stage brings together all the elements you need to process data at a specific point in a Pipeline. It is important to understand the difference between a Filter and a Stage. A Filter is an algorithm. It specifies a function (Bandpass Filter). It specifies the need for two Control Parameters (low- and high-frequency cutoff) and the need for a single pipeline profile input and output. A Stage, by contrast, represents the usage of a filter, with a specific purpose (Noise Filter) at a specific location (PCON-60) using specific Input Stage Parameter values (0.0, 3.3). Whereas a Filter may be referenced repeatedly and in more than one Pipeline, a Stage designates the usage of a Filter algorithm at a single Pipe Connection.

Here are the critical features of this improved object description:

1.  It defines *what* the object is.

2.  It explains *why* the object is a necessary concept.

3.  It explains *how* the object works.

4.  It uses diagrams and specific application examples.

5.  It makes reference to other parts of the model, which the reader must investigate to understand how all the pieces come together.

Of course, I wouldn't expect the whole model to make sense without a complete set of object, attribute and relationship descriptions. In fact, even the Stage object won't make complete sense out of context, but hopefully you get the idea.

The most important thing to remember is this:

**It is a waste of time to *merely* restate what is already obvious on the model.**

## Use both drawings and text

**Use drawings to communicate**
In the olden days - before desktop publishing became accessible to everyone - it wasn't always worth the effort to make pictures an integral part of documentation. Lack of artistic talent was another reason for relying exclusively on text to communicate. But those days are gone.

The tools are readily available for anyone, regardless of artistic talent, to interweave drawings with text. Why? Certain concepts are easier to communicate in a drawing than in a paragraph. Here is a classical demonstration of this principle: Try describing a spiral

using only words. Even if you can concoct a terse mathematical description, how many of your colleagues will instantly understand it? You can get the idea across a lot faster - to a wider variety of people - with a simple sketch. Naturally, the opposite is also true. There are many cases where text is superior to a diagram.

Usually some combination of text and diagrams yields the most useful descriptions. If you want to become an effective analyst, you must become skilled both in the use of technical drawing and word processing software.

**Use drawings to analyze**

Drawings aren't just for communication. The process of drawing, just like the process of writing, causes you to examine concepts in detail. But the process of drawing directs your attention to details different from those that you would notice while writing. Two weeks into a new project involving a semiconductor test machine, I discovered a critical safety error that no one else knew about. This all came about while I was producing a detailed diagram of how a robot arm moved around in an inspection chamber for an object description.

The diagram I was drawing incorrectly illustrated a mode of operation in which the human operator would have had his or her hand in the way of the robot arm while the robot was rehoming itself. One of the application engineers was explaining why my illustration was wrong when he realized that this particular scenario might actually be possible. After further investigation we found out that the bug really did exist.

**Illustrate physical objects**

It may not seem to be worth the time to illustrate physical objects. After all, physical objects are usually familiar to project members. If you are building a controller for a robot arm, it's not like you've got people on the team wandering around that don't know what the robot looks like. Even if someone hasn't seen the arm, they could just walk into the lab and take a look for themselves. If there aren't any robot arms in the lab, surely there is a picture in an operator manual somewhere.

Nonetheless, I've always found that it is worth the time to draw and describe most of the physical objects relevant to a domain. The process of drawing causes you to focus on details that are usually neglected. Drawings also go a long way toward clearing up confusion over terms. (This is especially important when you didn't realize that there was any confusion!)

Here's an application where a drawing of a common, well-known physical object (that no one wanted me to bother drawing) proved extremely useful.

APPLICATION NOTE

On one project we had a thing called a "stage," which served as a moveable platform for semiconductor wafers. People would use terms like "you put the wafer on the stage and move it to the load location," "you can rotate the stage," "you apply vacuum to the stage to hold the wafer down," "you can move the stage around manually," and so on. Frequently the term "chuck" was used instead of "stage". So you might "apply vacuum to the chuck," But there were odd differences. You "found the center of the chuck," but you never "found the center of the stage". The chuck had a diameter, but the stage didn't.

I resolved all this confusion by drawing and labeling pictures of the chuck and stage devices in the respective object descriptions. Here is the one for the chuck object:

## Chuck (CHK)

A Chuck is a short, wide, metallic cylinder designed to support a Wafer during inspection within a Station. A typical Chuck has a diameter of 20 cm and a height of 2 to 3 cm. Small holes in the Chuck surface allow a vacuum to be applied to the underside of a Wafer to hold it firmly in place.

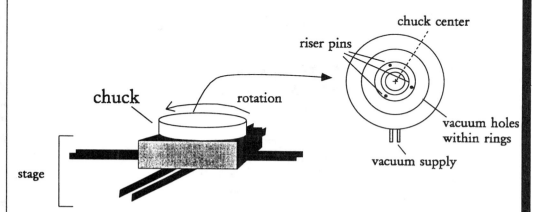

The Chuck rides on a Stage that can move the Chuck along multiple axes (see the Stage object for more about this). There are at least three different sizes (diameters) of Chuck to accommodate gross differences in Wafer size (15, 20 and 30 cm). When a new Chuck is mounted in a Station, it's a big deal - a technician has to recalibrate all the alignment parameters - a time-consuming process. Consequently, once a Chuck is installed, it tends to stay

Illustrated object descriptions of physical objects pay off in two ways. They resolve ambiguities in terminology and they highlight subtle physical features that otherwise would have gone unnoticed.

**Illustrate soft objects**     Soft (nonphysical) objects must also be illustrated. When you draw a physical object, you try to accurately render well-known and little-known but relevant features. Keen observation is the key to drawing physical objects. Soft objects, on the other hand, demand creativity. You may need to invent symbols. It can be a challenge sometimes to devise a useful way to visualize a nonphysical concept.

Here is an object description of a soft object:

## Step (STP)

A Step is a position within a Script where an Activity Specification may be attached. The only purpose of a Step is to establish the order in which Activity Specifications are normally executed. In an Archived Script acquired data is associated with the Step.

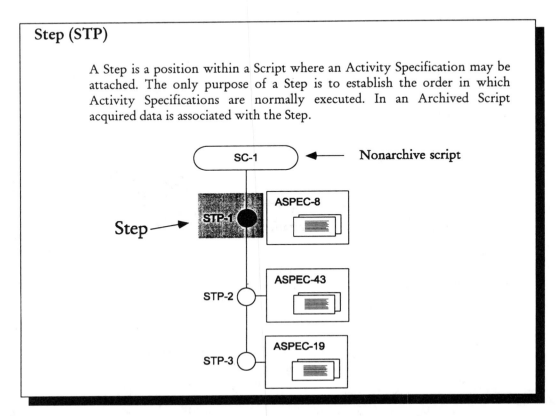

In this example, I invented symbols and labeled them with unique identifier values. The identifier value format is specified in the attribute descriptions of each object.

The process of drawing nonphysical objects almost always reveals holes in your thinking. (If not to yourself, then possibly to others!)

## Use terminology appropriate to the problem domain

If you are modeling within the application domain, stick to application terminology. If you are modeling within a service domain, stick to terms that make sense in that domain. For example, the terms "software" and "computer" shouldn't appear in descriptions within most application domains.

☹ A Pause is a point in time specified so that the software knows when to stop an animation.

☺ A Pause is a point in time where a running animation will stop temporarily.

It is okay to refer to "the system" (as long as the system is defined as an object somewhere).

☹ Only one Session can run at a time on the computer.

☺ The Scanning System can run only one Session at a time.

# Refer to other model elements in the same problem domain

You often need to explain an object in terms of how other objects, attributes and relationships are to be used. Here is an excerpt from an object description that explains how semiconductor wafers are transported.

> Once a Wafer is processed, it is moved according to the Transport Area's Active Route. The IS VISITED BEFORE relationship is used to find the first Process Site to visit that doesn't have a corresponding Completed Pass.

But don't overdo it. Explain just enough to put the object in context. The state and process models are the best place to describe dynamics in detail. Here is an example of overkill.

> Once a Wafer is processed, it is moved according to the Transport Area's Active Route. Get the Substrate.Current Location ID. Find the Transport Area that contains this Current Location. Get the Transport Area.Active Route. Find the last Completed Pass associated with this Route. Select it and find the Completed Pass.Process Site ID. Use the IS VISITED BEFORE relationship to access the Process Site.Next Process Site ID.

Yechh!

This example is thorough, but it tightens down the bolts way too soon. One little change in the information model and you have to rewrite the whole paragraph.

# Describe behavior

Some objects don't do much of anything. A specification object, for example, has a lifecycle like this: Create self, sit around and get referenced, delete self. The description of an object like this mostly describes the nature and utility of the object, rather than it's behavior.

But many objects have interesting behavior. It would be hard to describe the landing gear of an aircraft in an embedded control system, for example, without describing some of the primary states of the gear - retracted, retracting, extending, locked, and so forth.

Here is a soft object in a document version control system that requires a more detailed description of its behavior.

# Document in Revision (DIR)

A Document in Revision is a checked-out Document Version. Only a Document in Revision can be edited.

When an Internally Controlled Document is checked out by a Reviser, an instance of Document in Revision is created. Only one Document in Revision may be created for a given Document. In this way, two Revisers of a Document cannot get their hands on the same Document simultaneously.

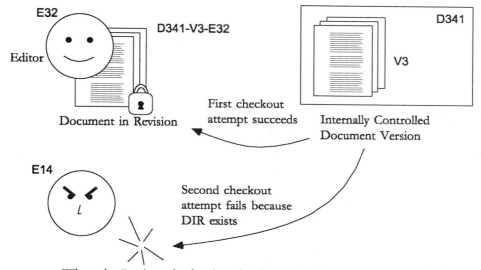

When the Reviser checks the edited copy back in, a new instance of Internally Controlled Document Version is created with an incremented Version Number. At this point the Reviser relinquishes control of the document and the instance of Document in Revision evaporates.

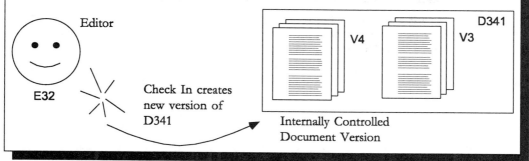

**Don't describe detailed behavior**

Don't waste time describing anything in the information model that would be better addressed in the state and process models. Statements like "then it sends an event to object X" and "this object communicates with object X" don't belong in an information model.

If you incorporate details of the dynamics in an object description, then your information will go out of date when you make changes in the state and process models. It's hard enough keeping the dynamic models up to date without having to keep coming back and changing the information model.

The situation you really want to avoid is where you spend so much effort describing what an object does that you forget to explain what the object means and why the object is required in the first place. Just because an object can be ascribed behavior doesn't mean that it is helpful or necessary.

# Don't be wishy-washy

Avoid watering down your descriptions with wimpy qualifiers like "generally," "usually" and "probably". Tentative descriptions keep you from learning anything new. It is better to use definite terms like "always," "never" and "must". When you are wrong, these words are 400,000-volt cattle prods that spark useful feedback from your otherwise laconic reviewers.

Imagine for a moment that you are an application engineer with a lot of expertise in the operation of an optical device inspection machine, the Flot-O-Scan 3000. Here is something you know about how flots[1] are inspected:

APPLICATION NOTE

> Flots are usually loaded into the inspection station in batches using a cartridge. Sometimes flots are loaded one at a time, using the manual feed tray. There is also an entry port at the rear of the station that can be used to manually load a single flot for diagnostic purposes.

Now read this phrase taken from the Flot Handler object description:

☹ A Flot is usually loaded from a Cartridge.

---

[1] Flot = flat optical device (see Figure 5.1 on page 77)

This statement is too wishy-washy. Maybe the analyst knows about the other two ways to load wafers and maybe he or she doesn't. Either way, this type of statement will not catch the application expert's eye.

Contrast it with a more direct statement:

☺ There are only two ways to load a Flot into the Flot-O-Scan. A Flot can be loaded one at a time using a Tray or in batches using a Cartridge. A Cartridge is used most of the time.

If you want the most up-to-date correct information, you must display your ignorance prominently. The direct statement (smiley face) is clearly false, and you can be sure that the application expert will straighten you out (assuming he or she actually reads it, but that's a different problem).

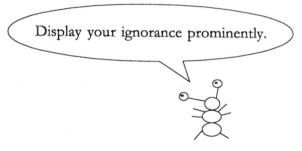

Of course, you can always intersperse your descriptions with parenthesized questions like (Is there any other way to load a wafer?). But that only works when you know that you might be wrong.

## How long should an object description be?

It depends on the object. Most objects take a page to describe, while others can be nailed down in three or four sentences. Some objects are so interesting that it takes two or three pages.

## How much explanation is necessary?

Sometimes it is difficult to know just how much needs to be explained when you are writing an object description. You have to assume that the reader is already knowledgeable to some degree about the technology on your project. If you are describing a robot arm, you don't have to write 20 pages on kinematics, although it might be helpful to cite any texts that are particularly relevant in an introduction to the information model.

To set the right level of explanation, it helps to picture some typical readers of your model. These are the most common reader profiles (not necessarily in order):

- Someone newly transferred or hired on to the project
- Other analysts
- Application experts
- Members of the design/implementation team
- You  (3 to 6 months later after you've returned from working on something else)

Assume that your reviewers are skeptical. If you make a nonintuitive abstraction, defend the reasoning behind it.

## Summary

An object description must answer the what, why and how questions. The process of answering these questions benefits the analyst as much as the reviewers.

Ninety-nine percent of the time an object description is read because the reader of your model got confused looking at the object symbol on the information model graphic. Write/draw your description with this scenario in mind. Your description should help remove that confusion as quickly as possible. So

- Use both text and drawings to define an object.
- Don't merely restate what is obvious on the model schematic.
- Use supporting examples.
- Make clear, decisive statements.
- Describe the essential behavior of an object, but don't describe state dynamics or object communication in any detail.

# Chapter 11   How to write attribute descriptions

At first, attributes can be a real pain to describe. With an attribute like Flot ID, for example, you may find yourself sitting in front of a mostly blank screen thinking, "Flot ID, hmm, The ID of a Flot - I mean, what else is there to say???" And yet there are issues associated with every attribute that must be documented. To avoid getting stuck, you need to be familiar with attribute categories.

**Attribute categories**

Having written lots of attribute descriptions, I've noticed that attributes fall into several loose categories. Within a given category, certain topics always need to be addressed. So if I can determine the category of an attribute, then I know what to write about (or at least what questions I need to ask). Often, I can copy a description from another attribute of the same category and then just modify it. Well, it's not quite that easy, but attribute categories do help you nail down those elusive descriptions.

Here is the list of categories and subcategories that I use.

- Descriptive attribute (color, time, mass, gain, name, x, y, z.)

    Subcategories: numeric, closed set, open set, semiclosed set

- Identifier attributes (session id, token id, catalog number, serial number)

    Subcategories: invented, found

- Referential attributes - single and grouped

These groups are rough classifications based on my experience writing and reviewing attribute descriptions. If you are trying to describe an attribute, use the guidelines and examples from that category as a starting point. If your attribute falls into more than one category, then you will have to merge the guidelines as appropriate.

The following format should be used with all attribute descriptions, regardless of category:

*attribute definition*

**elapsed travel time**   This is the amount of time that has elapsed since the Torpedo entered the FIRED state. This value is used to determine when to detonate the Torpedo or when to decide that the Torpedo should be considered lost and removed from the game.

*attribute name*

*Domain:* A positive real number of seconds.

*attribute domain description*

# Descriptive attributes

A descriptive attribute is an innate feature of an object. It is often a physical characteristic like dimension (x, y, z), orientation, time, color, shape, density, or location. Sometimes it represents capability limits like stall speed or maximum load. A name that cannot guarantee uniqueness (like employee name) is primarily descriptive.

## Descriptive attribute descriptions

**Use pictures**   Sometimes it is easier to illustrate descriptive attributes (especially dimensions) than it is to describe them in words. You'll see what I mean with the following description of a collection of attributes that define the path taken by a laser scanner:

If x1 is the left edge of the leftmost unit region that is covered at least partially by the infinite horizontal strip of height Scan Sweep Length with its top edge located at y = Ystart, and x2 is the right edge of the rightmost unit region satisfying the same criteria, then the width of the strip is given by | Xend - Xstart | = Acceleration Distance + (x2 - x2) + Deceleration Distance.

Whoa! My brain hurts. I think it's time to check my voice mail or something.

A picture like this makes the attributes easier to understand.

### Strip attributes

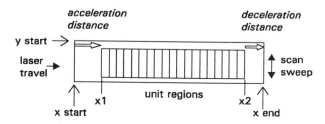

**Figure 11.1**

Ah yes. Now I feel much better.

Of course, you should augment the picture with some text and math, but my point is that pictures add a lot to attribute descriptions - so use them.

**Clarify the meaning of the attribute**

It is often impossible to divine the precise meaning of an attribute solely from its name. Clear up the specific meaning.

Submarine.Current Heading

This is the direction in which the Submarine is pointed (the Submarine may or may not be moving). Note that a Submarine that is applying reverse engines will have a Current Heading that is 180 degrees from its actual direction of motion.

# Descriptive numeric domains

**Don't be wishy-washy**

Here is a descriptive attribute with a tentative domain description.

Scanner.Power level

This is the amount of power applied to the infrared scanner. The value is provided as a control input to the scan control hardware.

☹ Domain: Some type of number (to be determined).

A domain description like this might be deferred for many reasons. Maybe the hardware design isn't complete. Maybe there is controversy as to whether the control will be a whole integer or a real number. Maybe the author of the model is worrying about more important problems. Or maybe the author is too lazy to track down the correct information.

If you review a model containing a domain description like this, you should find out why it is incomplete. If the author responds, "it's a design detail," then you know that the author is too lazy to track down the correct information. Nothing in the software design or implementation process will resolve the issue. One benefit of information modeling is that it brings to attention details that need to be nailed down. The analysis is not complete if the attribute domains are undefined.

In any event, I would rewrite the example domain description like this:

☺ Domain: An integer between 1 and 10 inclusive, where 10 is the maximum possible. Conversion of this value into milliwatts is performed by the hardware. (Walt - let me know if this changes.)

Here I am inventing a domain policy out of thin air. This statement will no doubt freak out the hardware folks. Admittedly, that's a little underhanded, but you've got to do something to get people to read your documents in sufficient detail.

The intent of a decisive description is to get the hardware engineers to make a decision, or at least to let them know that you are making default assumptions that may have to be corrected. This kind of writing may even help you to establish the hardware requirements that you want to see.[1]

**Measurements need units**

The following domain description is incomplete:

Reflecting Body.Distance

The distance from the sensor to the reflecting body.

☹ Domain: A positive real number

---

[1]In the long run you will get more respect from the hardware folks who think that software folks can never make up their minds.

A measurement doesn't mean anything unless it is defined precisely. Also, units should be specified when describing measurements.

The distance from the center of the sensor to the surface of the reflecting body.

☺ Domain: A positive real number expressed in meters.

In the second example, units are specified and distance is defined more precisely.

**Quantities don't need units**

With quantities, the units are reflected in the attribute name and the attribute definition, so the domain description need not specify units.

☺ Flot.Defect Quantity

The number of defects detected in the latest scan of this Flot.

Domain: A positive integer

**Specify precision when it is crucial to the application**

Most of the time precision is not specified because the implementation provides more than sufficient precision. But in some applications precision is a big issue. If this is the case, specify the precision demanded by the application - not the precision supplied by the implementation.

Tank.Pressure

☺ Domain: A real number in the range [ Tank Spec.Min Pressure, Tank Spec.Max Pressure ] to a precision of $\pm.01$ psi.

The square brackets indicate that the range is inclusive. By the way, it's perfectly okay to make reference to other attributes in a domain description. Just make sure that the statement is unambiguous and the referenced attributes are easy to find.

**Avoid implementation data**

Don't tell the programmer how to do his or her job.

Environment.Temperature

☹ Domain: A floating point value (implementation specific)

☺ Domain: A real number in the range from 0 to $\infty$ expressing kelvins.

**Coordinates**    Coordinates like x, y, z, q are common examples of descriptive attributes. Sometimes it is tempting to lump coordinates together.

☹ Grabber.Position

The location of the grabber.

Domain: Real numbers x and y expressing a distance in microns.

But this is bad practice because you can easily overlook important distinctions among the attributes that have been lumped together.

☺ Grabber.X Position

The position of the grabber on the X axis. This axis runs horizontally along the face of the machine. The grabber is moved along this axis to line up with one of the two loading robots.

Domain: A real number in the range [-37000, 37000] expressing microns. (An operator facing the machine has the negative extreme on his or her left. Zero is at the center of the front panel door.)

Grabber.Y Position

The position of the arm on the Y axis. This axis runs vertically from inside the inspection chamber to the top of the front panel. The grabber takes a sample from the load robot and brings it to the inspection chamber (and vice versa).

Domain: A real number in the range [0, 72355] expressing microns. (Zero is at the top of the front panel.)

**Specify the coordinate system**    All coordinates should be described with respect to a coordinate system. Here is an example from a user interface application.

☹ Cursor.X

Location on the X axis.

Domain: A real number in the range [-.5, .5].

Where is the X axis? Is the position relative to a specific window? the screen? Is distance measured in pixels or millimeters?

☺ Domain: A real number in the range [-.5, .5] expressing a location on the X axis in Normalized Device Coordinates. (See appendix for a description of the coordinate system.)

When a description applies to multiple attributes, you can put the information in an object description or in an introduction or appendix to the model. Diagrams are useful for showing how coordinate systems relate to one another.

**Internal constraints**      Sometimes a domain is restricted by the current value of some other attribute.

☺ Child Window.Lower Right X

Domain: A distance in pixels along the X axis from the left edge of the Parent Window. This value is a positive integer N such that Upper Left X < N < Parent Window.Lower Right X.

It's probably a good idea to say more about the attribute constraint in the attribute description (just before the domain description).

# Descriptive set attributes

With set domains, you have to be clear as to whether the set is open or closed.

**Closed set - Status**      Here is an example of a closed set domain:

Submarine.Pilot Mode

A Submarine may be controlled by either intermittently adjusting Dive, Rudder, and Engine settings or by establishing a Desired Speed, Heading, and Depth and switching the Submarine to autopilot mode. In autopilot mode, the game continuously adjusts the Dive, Rudder, and Engine settings as necessary to maintain the specified control set-points.

Domain: [ manual | autopilot ]

The [ | ] notation is taken from DeMarco[1] and indicates a closed list of choices. If you invent a new Pilot Mode setting like "Kamikaze" then you must update the attribute domain description.

---

[1] Tom DeMarco, *Structured Analysis and System Specification*, Yourdon Press, New York, 1978.

This is okay when you have simple modes like toggles. For more complex status attributes, the list of states changes every time someone updates the state model. Consequently, the reviewer should refer to the current state model for a complete list of states. Here is an example of how the domain description should be written:

Torpedo.Status

A Torpedo is created when it is loaded aboard a Submarine as a Stored Torpedo. A Stored Torpedo is prepared for use by loading it into a Torpedo Tube. The Stored Torpedo becomes a Loaded Torpedo at this point. This operation takes time since it requires the cooperation of a sometimes inexperienced or possibly hung-over crew. When a Loaded Torpedo is fired, it becomes a Fired Torpedo. The Fired Torpedo will rapidly hunt for its target or become lost. In either case the Fired Torpedo meets its end and is removed from the game.

Domain: A state like Stored, Loaded, Fired, and so on.

[Note: As this book goes to press, Sally tells me the current state of an object will no longer be captured as an attribute in the Shlaer-Mellor method. In that case, the contents of the two previous attribute descriptions should be included in the relevant object descriptions. The domain descriptions are unnecessary since they are simply the set of states in the corresponding state models.]

**Closed set - Types**    This kind of attribute usually refers to subtype object names. Here is an example where the domain of a type attribute corresponds to a set of subtypes.

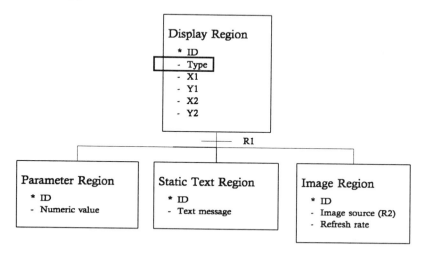

**Model 11.1**

Display Region.Type

This is the type of data that can appear in this Display Region. Only one type of data can be displayed in a single Display Region.

Domain: [ Parameter | Static Text | Image ]

If you add a new subtype to the information model, then you have to update the type attribute domain description. Since you are updating the information model anyway, this is not such a big problem.

**Open Sets**    Here is a case where the domain is a set, but it is impossible to specify a complete list of set members.

Cartridge.Process Sequence

The order in which Flots will be processed. An algorithm will be specified for each type of sequence.

Domain: An order like Top-Down, Bottom-Up, Middle-Out, Even-Odd, Random, etc.

In this case the domain is defined by example. Just be careful to add an "etc." at the end to make it clear that this is not intended to be a complete list. Otherwise, you put yourself in the position of having to update your model every time someone thinks of a new algorithm for processing Flots.

**Not quite so open sets**     With some set domains, it is not so easy to determine whether you should enumerate the domain or specify it using a numeric range. Here's the enumeration approach.

Flot.Thickness

The nominal thickness of a Flot. A number of standard Flot sizes are defined within the industry.

Domain: [ 5 | 10 | 20 | 25 ] mm

Contrast this with the range approach.

Domain: A real number > 0 expressing thickness in millimeters. Usually this is a standard size like 5, 10, 20, 25 mm. (range with a list of examples)

Both domain descriptions could be correct. We need to know more about the application. The following note argues for the enumeration (first) domain description:

APPLICATION NOTE

Flot sizes are based on an industry standard that is updated infrequently. You would like the system to recognize only the standard sizes. The user should be presented with a list of standard thicknesses to choose from. We don't want the user to type in just any number and then have to reject it or round it because the number is nonstandard.

But this note leads us to express the domain as a range (second domain description).

APPLICATION NOTE

> While it is true that the industry standard is updated only once a year, it is, nonetheless, updated. Also, what is to keep someone from fabricating a nonstandard flot for research purposes? True, you would still like to have the user choose from a list of standard flot sizes, but you would also like to provide an advanced option where a nonstandard size can be specified.

We have seemingly contradictory requirements. How do we model both restricted standard and unrestricted nonstandard flot thicknesses at the same time? Solution: Extend the information model using a specification object.

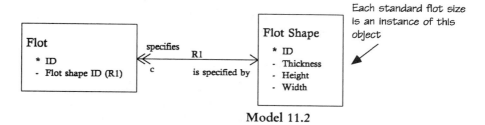

**Model 11.2**

**Constraining a domain with a specification object**

Here's how it works. First, you create instances for all the industry standard sizes in the Flot Shape object. The user interface restricts the user's selection to the current set of Flot Shape instances. If the user wants to define a nonstandard shape, a new instance must first be created in the Flot Shape object. The attribute domain of Flot Shape.Thickness becomes open ended.

☺ Domain: A real number > 0 expressing thickness in millimeters. Usually this is a standard size like 5, 10, 20, 25 mm. (range with a list of examples)

So we are restricting the domain of acceptable thicknesses explicitly using a set of instances in the Flot Shape object, rather than implicitly in the attribute domain description. The domain of Flot Shape.Thickness is properly expressed using a continuous range.

If the geometry of a Flot Shape were more complex (containing sophisticated internal features, for example), then you would need more than one specification object. In fact, you may uncover a whole subsystem's worth of specification objects.

# Descriptive name attributes

Naming attributes are often described as being nothing more than text strings. This is a bad practice.
Video Effect.Name

The user can assign string with arbitrary content to label a Video Effect.

☹ Domain: An ASCII string

Here is a more complete description that defines the purpose and usage of names without specifying an implementation.
Video Effect.Name

A user assigns a descriptive name to a Video Effect so that he or she can recognize the effect in the future. Names are not, however, guaranteed to be unique.

☺ Domain: Any name

The second domain description is better because it does not tell the programmer how to do his or her job. The use of ASCII strings might be a database or a software architecture requirement, but it is not an application requirement.

I am not just talking about a possible choice between ASCII or EBCDIC. Technology is changing fast. In future implementations, the name may be characterized by a bitmap or a list of phonemes.

## Identifier attributes

An identifier attribute is any attribute that forms all or part of an object identifier.

# Invented identifiers

An invented identifier is one that has been created by the analyst. In service domains - where you invent your own objects - invented identifiers are especially common. If you invented an object called Session, you would probably also invent a Session.ID to guarantee the uniqueness of instances in that object.

Sometimes identifiers are invented to supplant existing identifier schemes that do not guarantee full uniqueness or that consist of too many component attributes.

There really isn't much to say in the description of an invented identifier.

Session.Session ID

A unique identifier

Domain: SES < n >

The object abbreviation is followed by an integer ≥1, SES-32, for example. Since I use the same format for all invented identifiers, I describe the format only once in the introduction to the information model.

# Found identifiers

A found identifier is one that was already in use before you started the information model. If you are modeling parts sold in a catalog, for example, you might use the manufacturer's catalog number combined with the manufacturer code as a unique ID.

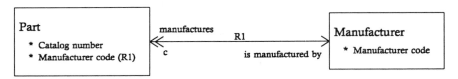

**Model 11.3**

Unlike the situation with an invented identifier, you are not in control. You are relying on some other source or mechanism for ensuring that the identifier values are unique. So you must justify the use of this outside source in the description.

Part.Catalog Number

A Manufacturer is responsible for assigning a Catalog Number to each Part that they sell. We haven't run across any cases where a Manufacturer duplicates a Catalog Number for the same Part. It is still possible that a duplication could occur, say a 4cm self-sealing stem bolt sold under two different Catalog Numbers. In this case, we would treat each Catalog Number as a separate Part even though each Catalog Number corresponds to the same product.

Part.Manufacturer Code (R)

The Part is built by this Manufacturer. Since two Manufacturers might use the same Catalog Number, we need to add the Manufacturer code as part of the identifier.

Domain: Same as Manufacturer.Manufacturer Code

In the Manufacturer object:

Manufacturer.Manufacturer Code

We assign a unique ID to each Manufacturer. This is usually the first three letters of the Manufacturer name. If two Manufacturers have the same three letters at the beginning of the name, then we will change one of the letters to make it unique.

194

The point is that you have to describe (1) why the source is a good choice as identifier or partial identifier (you must explain the rule or policy that guarantees uniqueness) and (2) explain any meaning behind the identifier (if one exists). One way to do this is by taking a case where you could end up with duplicate ID's and then explaining how that situation is avoided.

This practice often leads you to discover weaknesses in an existing identification scheme.

## Referential attributes

A referential attribute is any attribute native to some other object. It's existence formalizes part or all of at least one relationship.

## Referential attribute descriptions

Some common mistakes are made when describing referential attributes. Let's use this example taken from an application where Carriers (one of several types of containers) transport assemblies through a factory.

...

| Carrier | | Load |
|---|---|---|
| * ID | is contained in    R1    c | * ID |
| - Current location | c         contains | - Load type name |
| - Next location | | - Load priority |
| - Active move path | | - Current carrier ID (R1) |

**Model 11.4**

**Use the active voice**    Many times I find these written with bad grammar or in the passive voice.

Load.Current Carrier ID

☹ The Carrier it is currently in. (bad grammar)

But the grammatically correct alternative is awkward.

☹ The Carrier within which this Load is currently contained. (yechh!)

So I recommend that you flip-flop it and use the active voice.

☺ The Load is currently contained in this Carrier.

If the reviewer wants to know what a Carrier is, he or she can read the Carrier object description. In this example, the reason that Carrier appears in the Load object is summarized. A full explanation would presumably be found in the CONTAINS relationship description.

**Refer to the original description**

Now let's look at the domain description of Load.Current Carrier ID.

☹ Domain: CAR < n >

Don't redefine the attribute domain. Instead, refer to the original attribute definition.

☺ Domain: Same as Carrier.ID or None

If the relationship is conditional, don't forget to say that "none" is one of the possible values in the attribute domain description.

**Referenced attribute groups**

In Model 11.5, the Workstation object has a compound identifier consisting of the two attributes Workstation.ID and Cell.ID. The Workstation Queue references both of these two attributes to formalize the SERVES relationship.

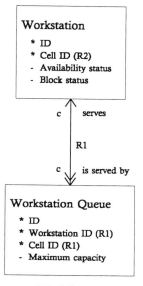

**Model 11.5**

Since both referential attributes serve the same purpose, you can lump them into a single description in the Workstation Queue object:

Workstation ID + Cell ID

The queue that serves this Workstation.

Domain: Same as Workstation.(ID + Cell ID)

*Chapter 12*

# How to write relationship descriptions

I'm not sure why, but objects seem to get all the attention. This is unfortunate because relationships are equally important. Many of the critical policies in an application are formalized by the naming, multiplicity and conditionality of the relationships. In fact, minor changes to a relationship can seriously alter the definition of the connected objects. Just as it does with objects and attributes, you will find that the careful definition of relationships almost always exposes errors in your logic (which, of course, is a good thing).

**Why relationship descriptions are neglected**

Here are some reasons why I think relationship descriptions are neglected:

1. Objects seem more tangible than relationships. What can you write about a relationship?

2. The object descriptions are generally written first. Once you write 15 or 20 object descriptions, you don't have much energy left over for the relationships.

3. The phrase "object-oriented" is taken much too seriously.

In this chapter, I hope to address reasons 1 and 2. Good luck with 3.

## What can you say about relationships?

As with any model description, you want to clear up confusion when you write about a relationship. To understand what to write, you need to understand where there is likely to be confusion. And what better place to find confusion than in someone else's model?

Take a look at any of the model examples in this book. Or go look at a model built by one of your colleagues. Are there any cases where the model would make a different statement about its application if the name, multiplicity or conditionality of one side of one of its relationships were to change? Are you confused about the exact meaning of the model because you can't tell what some of the relationships really mean? If you didn't answer "yes" emphatically, let the model sit on the shelf for a few weeks and try again.

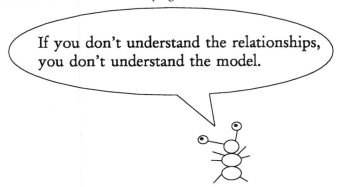

**If you don't understand the relationships, you don't understand the model.**

**Let's get confused**    Consider a factory management system. In this system we track process stations (factory machines) that apply operations like cutting, drilling and surfacing to a variety of materials. The process stations are organized into Station Groups. Let's take a look at one of the relationships in this application's information model.

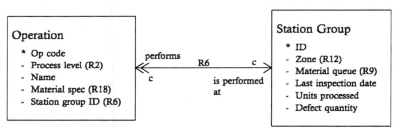

**Model 12.1**

Relationship R6 in Model 12.1 looks perfectly reasonable at first glance. But do we really know what R6 means? It says that a Station Group PERFORMS Operations. Does that mean at the present time? Can a Station Group perform multiple Operations at the same point in time? Or does R6 refer to configuration - a Station Group is configured to perform one of several Operations. Just because a Station Group has the capability of performing an Operation doesn't mean that the Operation is necessarily being executed at the moment. Or maybe the term PERFORMS means that a Station Group consists of machines that have the physical capability of performing a specific Operation. Are there any other possible interpretations of R6?

Okay, so we don't know the meaning of R6 - what about the multiplicity and conditionality? Model 12.1 says that an Operation is performed by zero or one Station Group. Why only one? Why can't multiple Station Groups perform the same Operation? If it is a consequence of the definition of Station Group - "a collection of Stations with the same capabilities" - then we should find out by looking at the Station Group object description. But the object description of Station Group wouldn't necessarily explain the circumstances when an Operation exists that is not performed by any Station Group. R6 also says that a Station Group might not perform any Operation. Why is that? Is it because a Station Group might exist that is not yet configured? Or is it because some Station Groups are not designed to perform machining Operations? If we knew the precise meaning of PERFORMS, we might be able to figure it out, but we don't.

**What every relationship description must contain**

Consequently, every relationship description should address the following:

- Its number, name, multiplicity and conditionality

- Its meaning

- Why it's 1 or M on each side

- Why it's conditional or unconditional on each side

- How it's formalized

Each of these items is present in the following example relationship description:

201

## Relationship descriptions

R6 - Operation IS PERFORMED AT Station Group (1c:Mc)
Station Group PERFORMS Operation

A Station Group can be set up to perform any number of Operations. Since all the Stations in a Station Group are always configured identically, Operations are defined for Station Groups - not individual Stations. The process of making a Station Group capable of performing any given Operation can require many preparation activities. It depends on the machinery and the machining process. Bits, dies or other fittings may have to be installed, programs and parameters may have to be downloaded, and operating conditions may have to be met.

A Station Group may be capable of performing multiple Operations. A wide variety of cutting Operations, for example, may be executed at the same machining station. (This is especially true at the new MeltBoy 9000 laser reducing station.)

During retooling, a Station Group is taken out of service and is therefore incapable of performing any Operations.

To simplify material transport, an Operation may be set up at only one Station Group. This does not affect throughput since there is no limit to the number of Stations within a Station Group.

An Operation can be defined by a manufacturing engineer without necessarily setting it up at a Station Group. This can happen when an Operation isn't needed for the current Run or when the corresponding Stations have not yet been installed.

Formalization: [ Operation.Station Group ID | none ]

Let's examine each component.

**The heading**    The heading displays the number and name of the relationship so that you can match it to the arrow on the graphic model. The name is stated from each direction so that you can prove to yourself and to others that the relationship makes sense from both points of view. As I write up the relationship, I usually find myself changing the name as I consider how it looks from each point of view. I tend to be more capricious when I jot the name down on the model graphic than when

I name it in the description. Sometimes this renaming process will make me realize that what I thought was a single relationship actually breaks down into two separate relationships.

The multiplicity and conditionality are stated just to be complete. Ideally, a CASE tool should fill in this information. We want to ensure that the descriptions contain a complete statement of the information model. If you throw the graphic part of the model away, you should be able to reconstruct the whole thing using only the descriptions.

**The meaning**

A relationship name alone can almost always be interpreted in more than one way. Your goal is not just to explain the meaning to other people, but to make sure that you really understand it yourself. Sometimes it helps to ask yourself when an instance of the relationship would be created or deleted. It often helps to draw a picture. Whereas instances of objects are often visualized as icons, instances of relationships can be represented several ways. Throughout the figures in this book, in fact, I have used the following methods to illustrate relationships: connecting lines, enclosed sets, relative proximity of object icons, and similar shading.

**Multiplicity and conditionality**

The multiplicity and conditionality nail down specific application policies. These policies often have subtle yet far reaching implications. Since these policies may not be evident to the model reviewer, you need to write down your reasoning. State the policy and use examples to justify the multiplicity and conditionality statements on each side of the relationship. In the example relationship description, there is a subtle policy that could be easily questioned. "To simplify material transport, an Operation may be set up at only one Station Group". This statement explains why the relationship is 1:M and not M:M.

It takes a lot of analysis effort to figure out where to put those little c's on the model graphic. They capture critical application policies. Imagine how you are going to feel weeks or months later when a colleague comes along and changes them without appreciating the implications. When you go to straighten him or her out about why the PERFORMS relationship is conditional on the Operation side, you find that you can't remember exactly why. All you remember was that there was lots of discussion and deliberation leading up to the decision to make it conditional. So you just stand there looking silly, confirming your colleague's suspicions that your model needs to be rethought.

So while you remember the reasoning, write it down.

**Formalization**  State which referential attribute(s) establishes the relationship. If you are using a good CASE tool, this should happen automatically.

## Don't write the relationship descriptions last!

One key to writing good, useful relationship descriptions is to interleave them with the object descriptions. If you put all the relationship descriptions in a separate document, you will probably end up doing them last. Here is a generic outline of how I organize my model descriptions so that the relationships don't get the short end of the stick.

> Object A
>
>> Object description
>
> Attribute descriptions
>
>> Attribute A
>>
>> Attribute B
>
> Relationship descriptions (if any)
>
>> Relationship A
>>
>> Relationship B
>
> Object B (new page)
>
>> ...and so forth

Each object starts on a new page. In the relationships section I choose any of the relationships connecting to the described object when this object seems to be the main participant. If a relationship is already written up as part of another object description, then I just skip it. If all the connected relationships are covered elsewhere, then this section is omitted.

I put a relationship index up front so that reviewers know which object to look under to find a given relationship.

When you write up the object description, you usually start thinking about some of the relationship rules. Since the relationship section is right there at the bottom of the page, you can easily skip down, fill in the details, and then jump back up to the object description. When you finish the object description, the relationship descriptions at the bottom are pretty easy to finish up because you've already filled in the meaty parts. It makes the description process much more natural than the alternative. I mean... think about it. Doesn't it seem a little odd to describe all the objects in one pass and then to describe all the relationships?

## Summary

Well, that's it. If you write descriptions that expose detailed application policies - that expose your thinking - then your models will improve dramatically.

# Model patterns

3

# Chapter 13

# Is zero-one-many specific enough?

The Shlaer-Mellor method gives you a notation for modeling relationships involving zero, one or many instances. But no notation is provided to constrain the cardinality of a relationship to a specific number.

This might seem strange, since numeric limitations appear frequently in requirements and in the real world in genral. If you know, for example, that your system will have two DSP's (digital signal processors) on every board, why not make the many arrowhead more precise by sticking a 2 symbol next to it, as shown below?

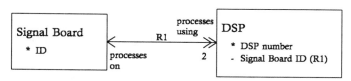

**Model 13.1**

**Why Shlaer-Mellor doesn't use numbers**

First, let's review the reasons why this issue doesn't come up with most relationships.

1.  The logic that handles three instances shouldn't be any different from the logic that handles four instances, so why bother with numbers?

2.  The logic that handles zero instances is often different from the logic that handles one or more instances, so distinguishing 1, 1c, M and Mc is important.

3.  A data structure that might reference multiple instances will probably be designed differently than a data structure that is guaranteed to reference exactly one instance.

4.  A requirement with a number in it is likely to change (today we absolutely will have two DSP's on each board - next month it could be three).   This is the kind of change that should be han-

209

dled in the data values, not the coded structures of your system.

5.  Many relationships are dynamic, so they can only be characterized qualitatively, not quantitatively.

Reason 4 is enough to keep me from quantifying the DSP relationship example.

**A case where zero-one-many isn't enough**

But consider this example:

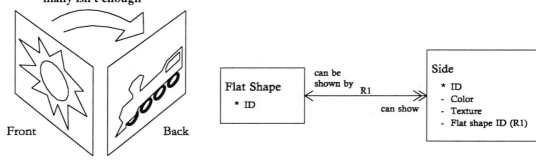

Front          Back

**Model 13.2**

Here we have a Flat Shape in a graphic animation system that can have a different bitmapped image painted on each side. We could model it as shown here, but a few realities nag at us.

*   A Flat Shape has two sides and planar geometry isn't likely to change. So much for reasons 4 and 5.

*   If we were to code this in C, let's say, the structure would probably incorporate this numeric fact. For example,

```
struct flatshape
{
        struct side front;
        struct side back;
}
struct side
{
        int color;
        int texture;
}
```

There goes reason 3 (reasons 1 and 2 generally follow 3 right out the window).

So the argument for modeling the two-ness of a planar shape is compelling. But can you do it using Shlaer-Mellor without inventing new notation?

**An attempt at modeling two-ness**

We could try using two one-to-one relationships to more precisely enforce two-sidedness:

(Not quite right)

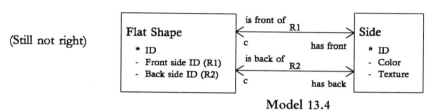

**Model 13.3**

This model says that a Flat Shape has both a front and a back Side. But it also says that a Side is both the front and back side of a Flat Shape. No good. A Side is either the front or back of a Flat Shape.

Can we fix it by making the relationships conditional?

(Still not right)

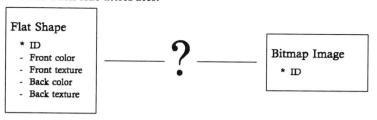

**Model 13.4**

Now the model says that a Side might exist that doesn't belong to any Flat Shape. Still no good.

We could try solving the problem with attributes instead of relationships. Since a Flat Shape always has two sides, why not just give it front and back side attributes?

```
Flat Shape
  * ID
  - Front color
  - Front texture
  - Back color
  - Back texture        ?        Bitmap Image
                                   * ID
```

**Model 13.5**

This model ensures that every Flat Shape has exactly two sides, so it seems to accurately model the application. But we need the Side object to model relationships between a specific side and the Bitmap Image object.

This leads us back to Model 13.4.

**The trick is to abstract the positional roles as objects**

When you keep staring at the same handful of objects and relationships without arriving at a solution, it sometimes means that you have the wrong objects. Consider breaking the Side object down into Front and Back Sides. This may seem silly, because a Front Side behaves exactly the same way as a Back Side. But there is a relative difference when they are attached to a Flat Shape. This relative difference can be captured by modeling the Front/Back roles played by a Side using subtypes.

Now we can make statements about Sides in general by building relationships to the Side object. We can make rules about Front Sides that may be different from rules about Back Sides. It is not clear that we need this flexibility, but it won't hurt either. As you can see below, it does solve our relationship problem

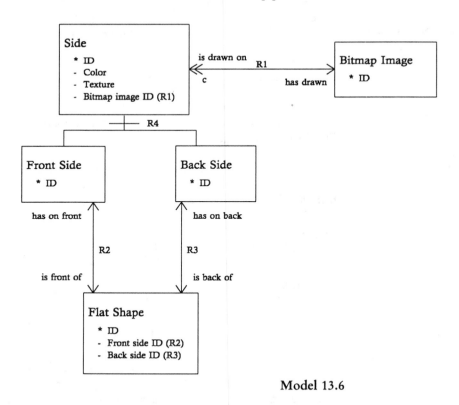

**Model 13.6**

This model says that a Flat Shape has exactly one Front Side and exactly one Back Side. It also says that a Front Side is always on exactly one Flat Shape and that a Back Side is always on exactly one Flat Shape. Success!

Now that we have the real world modeled, we can do a bit of house-keeping on our model. The following model is logically equivalent and a bit tidier:

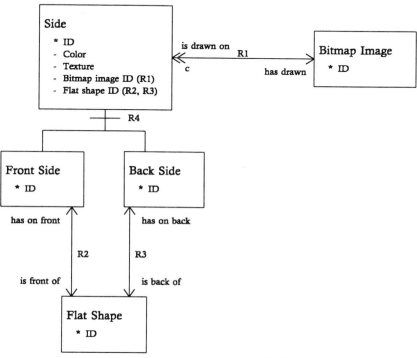

**Model 13.7**

Since relationships R2 and R3 are each 1:1, I was able to have the Sides refer to the Flat Shape, instead of the other way around. This gave me two referential attributes, Front Side.Flat Shape ID (R2) and Back Side.Flat Shape ID (R3). But since these two references share the same attribute domain, I let the Side supertype inherit them as the single attribute, Side.Flat Shape ID (R2,R3).

# Conclusions

If you find yourself in a situation where you want to model the two-ness or three-ness of a relationship, first consider how strongly the numeric constraint is enforced in the real world. If the constraint is important because someone put it in boldface in the requirements document, then (in my experience) it is subject to change and not worth modeling. But if it is a fundamental law of geometry, math, physics, or some other relevant field, then it is probably worth embedding in the structure of your system. If that is the case, then consider the different roles played by the two or three things relative to one another. Use subtypes to model these roles.

# Chapter 14       Reflexive patterns

A reflexive relationship is a relationship drawn on a single object like this:

This type of relationship abstracts associations among instances of the same object. The basic characteristics of this type of relationship were introduced at "Reflexive relationships" on page 72.

## Reflexive relationships and graphs

Reflexive relationships are necessary whenever you encounter a bunch of things - all of the same type - that systematically associate with one another. Consider some examples: a network of hypertext links (Link CAUSES NAVIGATION TO Link), a linear sequence of destinations to be visited by a robot (Destination IS VISITED AFTER Destination), and a hierarchy of relative coordinate systems (Coordinate System DEFINES SPACE RELATIVE TO Coordinate System).

These examples correctly suggest that associations among instances of the same object can always be drawn as some type of graph.

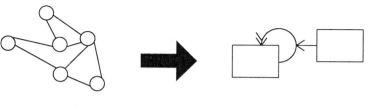

Network of
instances

Abstracted
network pattern

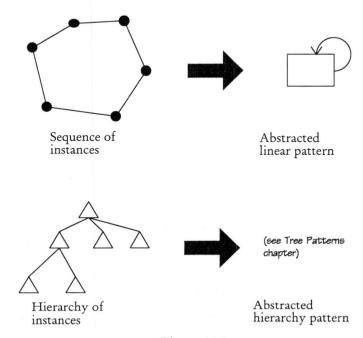

Sequence of
instances

Abstracted
linear pattern

Hierarchy of
instances

Abstracted
hierarchy pattern

**Figure 14.1**

When you model an object that references itself, you are modeling a graph. Fortunately, graphs are well studied things. A discrete math book will provide you with a list of common graph types (networks, trees, lists, etc.) and graph properties (cyclic, acyclic, connected, directed, multiedged, etc.). The accuracy, precision and completeness of your self-referencing relationship depends on how thoroughly you have addressed the relevant properties of the type of graph that you are modeling.

Let's say, for example, that you have just drawn a model of communication channels opened between processes on a computer:

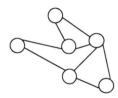

A familiarity with common graph properties will prompt questions like: Does this model allow processes with no communication channels (unconnected)? Processes that communicate with themselves (cycles)? One-way versus two-way communication (directed)? As you answer each of these questions you must make appropriate refinements to the model.

**Modeling graph constraints**

You probably won't get (or haven't gotten) very far in an application before you find yourself trying to model associations conforming to one of the graphs in Figure 14.1. I can tell you from painful experience that graphs are not always easy to formalize in an information model. This is especially true when the application permits instances in the graph to be created and deleted during runtime by a human user. The more dynamic the associations among instances is, the more precise the constraints that must be formalized. Of course, you can always wimp out and leave all the constraints to be enforced in state model actions. Have fun debugging.

**Reflexive models can be trivial**

Here's the good news. The typical reflexive relationship can be modeled with a straightforward one-object, one-relationship solution. This type of solution permits potentially illegal or nonsensical associations, but that's okay if instances are either (1) manually instantiated prior to runtime by an engineer (as is often the case with specification objects) or (2) managed by a conservative set of operations.

**Reflexive models can get ugly**

When a graph - even an apparently simple graph - needs extensive constraints, you may spend weeks deriving a sophisticated arrangement of objects and relationships that does the job.

**But don't worry**

In the next few chapters, we will look at several ugly self-referencing scenarios that I've modeled myself into (and out of). The resulting models formalize reflexive patterns that I've seen resurface in several otherwise disparate applications. These are the same patterns sketched in Figure 14.1. Hopefully, you will get some use out of these models.

Before moving on, however, I want to address a source of confusion that often muddies the waters of reflexive relationship modeling. Oddly enough, experience designing self-referencing code structures can hinder the modeling of reflexive application policies as much as it helps. To build good models, you must recognize the difference between reflexive policies inspired by implementation needs and those that are truly essential to the application.

# Self-referencing in analysis and programming

The reflexive concept - the idea that a thing can reference another thing of the same type - is encountered both in analysis and programming. Your goals, however, are different in each activity. I will point out the differences so that the programming goals (which are perfectly reasonable when you are programming) don't become intertwined with your analysis goals.

**Isn't self-referencing an implementation concept?**

It might be argued that lists, trees and other types of graphs are implementation ideas that belong in program code and not in the information model of an application. That depends.

Take a factory application, for example, where bar coded Trays are transported single file on a Conveyor Belt.

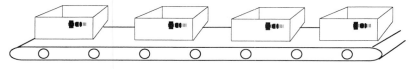

**Figure 14.2**

The fact that Trays are sequenced is an application fact. It is not a computer software fact. Consequently, we must formalize the sequencing of Trays in an information model - just as we would formalize any other application fact:

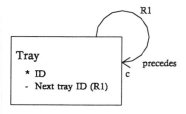

**Model 14.1**

You will use some kind of self-referencing code structure to implement the application fact formalized by Model 14.1. One possibility is a doubly-linked list:

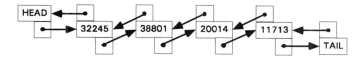

**Figure 14.3**

The information model states that Trays relate to one another in a linear fashion. Period. No determination is made that a linked list will be used and, if it is, whether it will be singly or doubly linked. The choice of single or double linkage is based on factors like the time it takes to traverse a list, the storage requirements of the list and the complexity of managing the list. Or maybe an array will be used instead (or in combination). The analyst does not care. The programmer is required, however, to employ a mechanism that somehow implements the fact that Trays follow one another on a conveyor belt.

**Like all relationships, a reflexive relationship can be viewed from two perspectives**

The Next Tray attribute in Model 14.1 formalizes the PRECEDES relationship. Since the multiplicity of the relationship is one-to-one, we can choose to put the referential attribute on either side of the relationship. This would make sense in a nonreflexive relationship where we have two participating objects. But since we have only one object, the choice is more subtle. If we imagine the attribute on one side of the relationship, we get "Next Tray". On the other side of the relationship (but in the same object), we get "Previous Tray". As with any relationship having one-to-one multiplicity, the choice is arbitrary.

Let's stick with "Next Tray". Now choose an arbitrary instance of Tray, T212 let's say. Can you find the next Tray on the conveyor belt? Sure. Just select the instance whose identifier matches the value of T212's Next Tray attribute. If none exists, we assume that T212 is at the last one on the conveyor belt. How about the other way around? Can you find the Tray behind T212? Yes. Just select the instance of Tray that refers to T212 - if it exists. Nonreflexive 1c:1c relationships work the same way.

The process of instance selection just described might sound inefficient, but that's the way the relational formalism works. If you want to speed things up, then use an architecture that translates each 1c:1c relationship into an appropriate optimized data structure. During implementation we are concerned about how the data is accessed. In analysis we are concerned only with what things are related and why they are related.

## Implementation mechanisms disguised as application policy

Sometimes the distinction between application and implementation structures is subtle. Consider the following example taken from a semiconductor wafer test program. Here is a picture of a Wafer that will have each of its dies probed and tested.

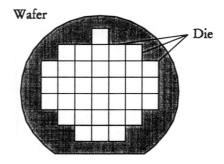

Figure 14.4

A numeric test code is returned for each die. Further action will be taken based on the value of this test code, as shown in the table below. This table data structure was extracted from program code written for the wafer test application:

Test result action table

| Test Code | Ink | Retest | Skip |
|-----------|-----|--------|------|
| 0 | Y | N | N |
| 1 | Y | N | N |
| 2 | N | Y | N |
| 3 | N | N | Y |
| . | . | . | . |
| . | . | . | . |
| . | . | . | . |

Sample data has been entered for a range of test codes. The actions are:

- Ink: paint an ink spot on the presumably defective die.

- Retest: test the die again.

• Skip: do nothing, move on to the next die.

Given the task of reengineering this application, a novice analyst might construct the following model...

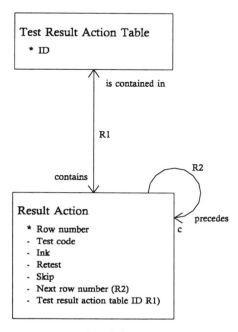

**Model 14.2**

which uses a reflexive relationship to capture the test result action table structure. But this model adds no analytic insight to the application.

The following model is better:

**Model 14.3**

because it doesn't attempt to model the programmer's data structure choice. It captures the requirement that actions be prescribed for different test results as minimally as possible. As a consequence, some faults in the programmer's design decision are avoided.

1.  Mutually exclusive actions can be avoided. The "skip" action, for example, is handled by not making any instances of R1 for a given Test Result.

2.  New acti ns, "scratch" instead of "ink", for example, can be added without changing the information model.

Before modeling a reflexive structure, make sure that you are modeling essential application policy and not an artificially imposed structure.

# Simple and complex graphs

The following chapters are organized in order of ascending graph complexity. A network graph (Chapter 15) has relatively few constraints to enforce and so it is easily modeled. List and tree graphs (Chapter 16) and (Chapter 17), on the other hand, present some intriguing modeling challenges.

# Chapter 15

# Network patterns

A many-to-many reflexive relationship models things that associate with one another in a networked fashion. This chapter explores two such things, adjacent territories on a map and networked computer processors. As we shall see, a single model pattern does not work for all types of networks. The model must be carefully sculpted to precisely match the details of the application.

## Adjacent territories

The board game of Risk[1] splits a continent up into a number of territories.

Venezuela

Adjacent territories
in the Risk board game

Brazil

Peru

Argentina

**Figure 15.1**

In this game, armies in one territory are allowed to attack the armies in any adjacent territory. Two territories are adjacent if they share a common border. Every territory on the board is adjacent to at least

---

[1]Risk® is a registered trademark of Parker Brothers.

one other territory. Island territories are connected to bordering territories with dashed lines. Madagascar, for example, is considered to be adjacent to East Africa and South Africa.

**No islands, acyclic**

The rules are:

- A territory is adjacent to any number of other territories.

- A territory cannot be adjacent to itself (no cycles - acyclic).

- Each territory is adjacent to at least one other territory.

This leads us to the following model:

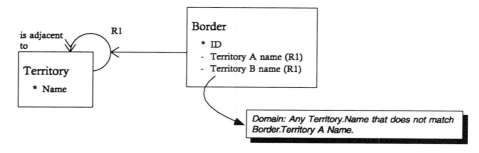

**Model 15.1**

Territories are next to each other; there is no role distinction like parent/child, positive/negative or above/below. It is therefore necessary to make an arbitrary distinction in the attribute name like A/B, as I did with the Territory referential attributes in the Border object.

**Making a relationship acyclic**

The IS ADJACENT TO relationship is unconditional, so every Territory must border at least one other Territory. To prevent a Territory from bordering itself, the domain of Border.Territory B Name is constrained so that it never matches Border.Territory A Name.

One nice thing about this model is the way the Border object arises so cleanly out of the associative relationship.

Now let's move on to a less constrained network pattern.

**Communicating processes**

Consider computer processes that open and close communication channels with one another. When a channel is opened, it provides for the two-way exchange of messages between the connected processes. Here is a possible configuration.

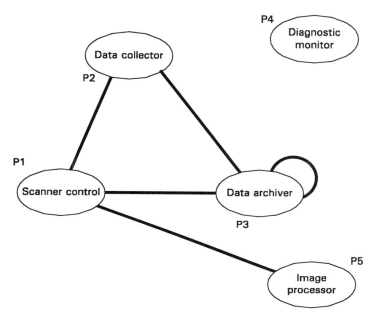

**Figure 15.2**

**Cycles, islands, and single connections**

Before jumping to the information model, let's make sure we have the rules straight:

- A channel is two-way (nondirectional).
- A process can open a channel with any other process.
- A process can even open a channel to itself (cycles ok - why not?).
- A process might have no channels open.

The following model captures our list of rules:

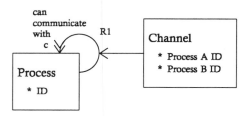

**Model 15.2**

A Process establishes communication with another Process, or with itself, by creating an instance of Channel.

In mathematical terms, we have just modeled an undirected, cyclic graph.

**Cycles, islands, and multiple connections**

What if we want to open two Channels between a pair of Processes?

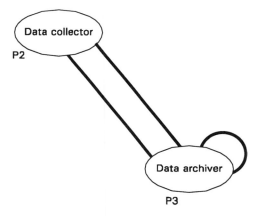

**Figure 15.3**

We need to incorporate the following rule into our model:

- Multiple Channels may share the same source and destination points.

But Model 15.2 doesn't accommodate multiple connections between the same source and destination.

This limitation is apparent if you try to fill out a table of Channel instances like the following:

| A PID | B PID |
|-------|-------|
| P1    | P2    |
| P1    | P3    |
| P1    | P5    |
| P3    | P3    |

**Table 15.1**

The associative relationship is 1-Mc:Mc. This means that for every instance of the CAN COMMUNICATE WITH relationship, there is exactly one instance of the Channel object. The A Process ID and B Process ID attributes are combined to form the Channel identifier. We can't have two Channel instances with the same identifier values (P2, P3) in this case. Model 15.2 limits us to one Channel between any pair of Processes.

**A,B and B,A mean the same thing**

Now you might argue that the identifier values (P2, P3) are distinct from the identifier values (P3, P2) so that you could have at most two Channels between a pair of Processes. But that's cheating. Process ID A and Process ID B describe arbitrary roles so there is no semantic distinction between P3, P2 and P2, P3. When you create an instance of Channel, (P3, P2) let's say, you must always check to ensure there is no instance of P2, P3.

To create a semantic distinction, you could change the names A/B to From/To. Then the instances (From P2, To P3) and (From P3, To P2) would mean different things. But that makes the Channels directional, and our list of rules did not specify directional Channels.

**Directional and multiple**

We need to clarify our rule. Why do we want to allow multiple Channels? Is it to make our Channels directional? Or do we just want multiple nondirectional Channels? Each answer demands a different information model solution. Let's take a look at the directional solution first.

**Making the graph directional**    Here is a directional configuration.

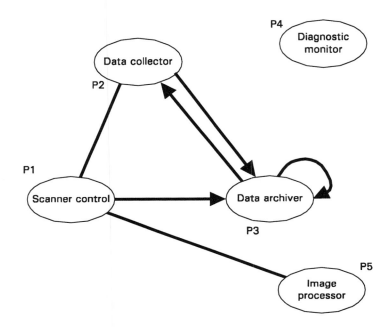

**Figure 15.4**

And here are the new rules:

- A Channel permits the passage of data in one direction only.

- There may be no more than one Channel in any given direction between the same two Processes.

Here is a model that formalizes these rules.

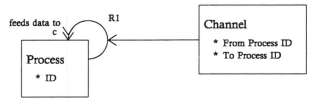

**Model 15.3**

The relationship name is reworded to make it directional - FEEDS DATA TO. The referential attributes in the Channel associative object are no longer A/B. The From and To modifiers indicate the direction of the relationship.

You can see how the Channel table subtly changes.

| From PID | To PID |
|----------|--------|
| P1 | P2 |
| P2 | P3 |
| P3 | P2 |
| P1 | P5 |
| P3 | P3 |

**Table 15.2**

Since there is a semantic difference between From and To, we can consider P2, P3 to mean something different than P3,P2.

But what about P3, P3?

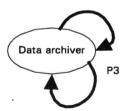

**Figure 15.5**

The above situation is not allowed by Model 15.3 because we can have only one instance of Channel with the (P3, P3) identifier. But that's probably okay, because if a Process is sending data to itself, an extra Channel isn't necessary for two-way communication. If there is some need for multiple loops on a single Process, directional or otherwise, we need to explore the idea of multiple Channels further.

**Multiple nondirected Channels**

Let's say we want to allow multiple two-way Channels between Processes like this:

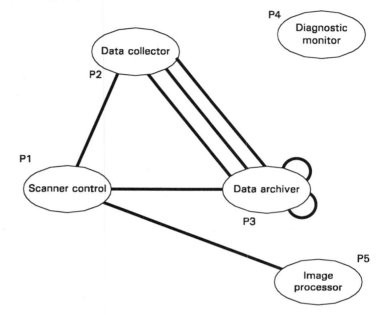

**Figure 15.6**

The new rules are:

- Any number of Channels may be opened up from one Process to another (or to the same process).

- Channels are not directed.

Here is the new model:

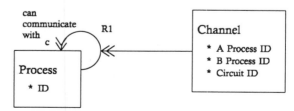

**Model 15.4**

This is a M-Mc:Mc relationship, which means that for every instance of CAN COMMUNICATE WITH there are one or more instances of Channel. But to pull this off we need to add a third component to the Channel identifier.

Let's see how this looks in a table.

| From PID | To PID | Circuit ID |
|----------|--------|------------|
| P1 | P2 | C1 |
| P2 | P3 | C1 |
| P2 | P3 | C2 |
| P2 | P3 | C3 |
| P1 | P3 | C1 |
| P1 | P5 | C1 |
| P3 | P3 | C1 |
| P3 | P3 | C2 |

**Table 15.3**

With the addition of Circuit ID to the Channel identifier, there can be as many loops as we like on a single Process.

**Multiple directed Channels**

To model one-way Channels, we just change (once again) A/B to From/To as shown:

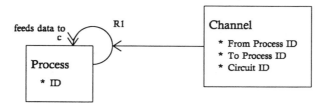

**Model 15.5**

**Bidirectional Channels**

Model 15.5 supports multiple directional Channels. But maybe all we want are bidirectional Channels. Can we constrain Model 15.5 somehow?

Specifically, we want to capture these rules:

- A Channel is one way.

- There can be no more than one Channel for each direction of communication between two Processes (or the same Process).

Up to this point, we have handled added constraints and features with slight modifications to a basic model. But clever attribute naming and placement of those little **c**'s only gets you so far. We need to think about the problem a new way.

For example, we could think about Channels as coming in two flavors.

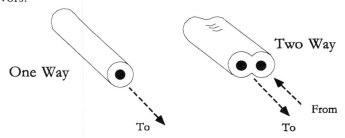

**Figure 15.7**

Let's model this new concept.

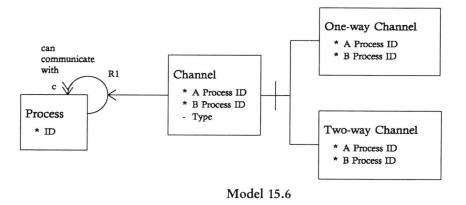

**Model 15.6**

This model says that between any two Processes (or the same Process) there may be one Channel. The Channel provides either one-way or two-way communication.

232

Let's see how the following Channel instances

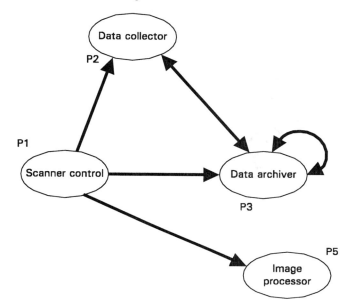

**Figure 15.8**

appear in a table:

| A PID | B PID | Type |
|-------|-------|---------|
| P1 | P2 | One Way |
| P2 | P3 | Two Way |
| P1 | P3 | One Way |
| P1 | P5 | One Way |
| P3 | P3 | Two Way |

**Table 15.4**

While this model accommodates the stated rules, it doesn't model the data flow inside a Channel. When we thought about a Channel as being a one-way flow of communication, that wasn't a problem. Both the data flow and the Channel were pretty much the same thing. But this is not the case with a Two-way Channel.

What if you wanted to attach a message to a particular data flow during runtime?

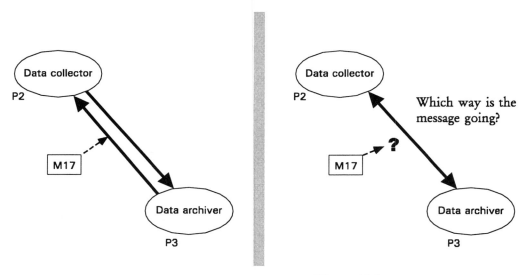

**Figure 15.9**

Let's see if we can extend our model to handle this situation.

**Separating Channel from Data Flow**

We need an object that represents communication in a single direction. We will call this object a Data Flow. The connection between two processes (or the same process) will still be referred to as a Channel. We want to say that a Channel consists of one or two Data Flows.

This leads us to the following model:

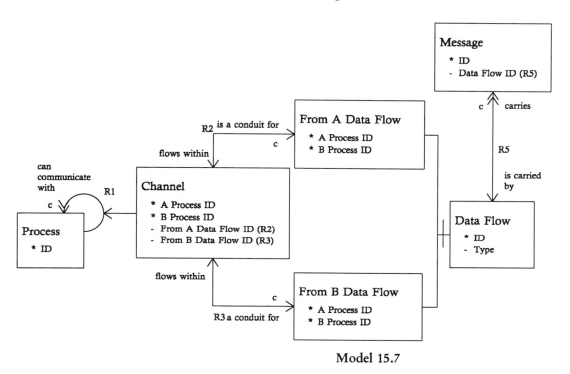

**Model 15.7**

**Subtyping by role**  You might be uncomfortable seeing From A Data Flow and From B Data Flow as separate objects. After all, each type of Data Flow behaves the same way. I am supposed to be modeling the real world, not introducing artifacts just to make my model work.

But I am modeling the real world. The Data Flow subtypes are differentiated by the roles that they play. Positive and negative wires function similarly, but we distinguish them with different words, symbols and colors. Is that real enough!?

Model 15.7 says that a Channel contains a From A Data Flow, a From B Data Flow, both types, or neither. I picked the names From A/ From B for the Data Flow subtypes. You might prefer A Out/B Out, From A/To A, or even Positive/Negative. Consistency is the important thing.

Now we have the Data Flow object to which we can attach a Message. This lets us specify which way a Message is going.

# Summary - really important stuff

In this chapter we modeled cases where many things connect to many things; nondirectionally, unidirectionally and bidirectionally. The following techniques were helpful:

- Draw tables and fill in instances to verify that you aren't breaking the model formalism (table rules) and to visualize how the abstract model handles tangible instances.

- Draw pictures and think up alternative paradigms (like the two-way channel concept) to transform a difficult modeling problem into a trivial modeling problem. You may not be able to change the application requirements, but you might find a different way to think about the application so that it is easier to model. Informal, nonmodel drawings (like Figure 15.7) are indispensable to this rethinking process.

**Important advice about using patterns**

There is more to modeling a network than just selecting a self-referential many-to-many relationship from your repertoire of model patterns. Pattern selection usually amounts to a good start. To develop an adequate model, you need to carefully inventory the application rules and verify that each rule in your list is captured by the model. Your initial pattern will cause you to ask more detailed questions about the application. The answers to these questions will almost always necessitate adjustments to the initial model. At best, you may need to change an attribute name or two. At worst, you may uncover application policies that mandate serious modeling effort. In either case, this additional effort will add valuable insight into the application.

*Chapter 16* Linear patterns

In this chapter we will look at different ways to model linear patterns such as

- items in a queue,

- a list of commands in a script,

- a physical sequence of se,nsors, actuators or the like,

- control points in a spline, and

- a data filter pipeline.

All these applications look like they can be handled with a model like this

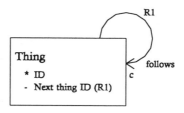

**Model 16.1**

which is definitely a good place to start. Upon closer examination, you may find that the application requirements require a more sophisticated model. We will model two or three linear patterns as precisely as possible. I plan to demonstrate two things:

1. How thoroughly you can capture rules and exceptions in an information structure.

2. It can take many objects and relationships to precisely model a simple list!

# Example 1: Mission editor in a flight simulator

To start off, I will use an application problem taken from flight simulators on personal computers.[1] The more sophisticated flight simulators give you the capability to preprogram the movement of air and ground units. As you fly your plane around in the flight simulator, you can observe activity in the air and on the ground. Looking at the ground, you might see a bunch of tanks moving in one direction where they will encounter several enemy tanks coming from another direction. Looking ahead you see a squadron of enemy planes going northeast and then turning south to support the enemy tanks.

To program all this activity, you call up a mission planning editor. Here you can plan routes for various types and quantities of battle units. These routes are laid out on a battlefield that might look like this:

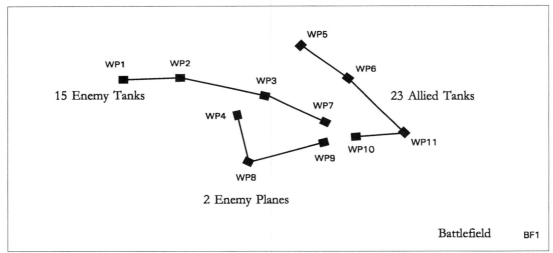

**Figure 16.1**

In this battlefield, separate converging routes have been planned for a group of 15 enemy tanks, 2 enemy planes and 23 allied tanks.

A square represents a Waypoint where a new heading is specified. The legs drawn between Waypoints illustrate the movement of the associated battle units. When the game is initiated, the battle units will move along these legs.

---

[1] Well, that's one of the reasons this book took so long to write...

**Connecting the waypoints**       Let's model the waypoints and the battlefield first:

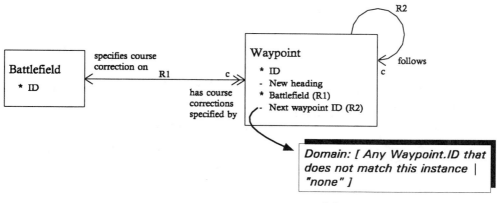

**Model 16.2**

This model says:

- Zero, one or many Waypoints may be specified on a Battlefield (R1)..

- A Waypoint may or may not follow another Waypoint (R2).

- A Waypoint cannot follow itself (attribute domain description of Next Waypoint ID).

- One Waypoint can follow another Waypoint only if they are both on the same Battlefield (formalization of R2 using a partial reference that excludes Battlefield ID).

All these rules agree with our sketch in Figure 16.1. The FOLLOWS relationship is conditional to allow for the first Waypoint (which does not follow a Waypoint). But this conditionality also makes it possible to specify a completely independent Waypoint. Is that okay? Sure. A tank at a single Waypoint would stay put; a plane at a single Waypoint would maintain a hold pattern.

**Adding battle units to follow the Waypoints**

Now let's add the battle units. We need to know which Waypoints are to be visited by enemy tanks and which are to be visited by allied planes.

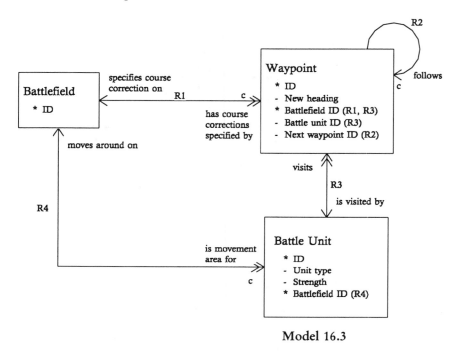

**Model 16.3**

This model ensures that:

- Every Waypoint is assigned to only one visiting Battle Unit (R3).

- A Battle Unit moves around on exactly one Battlefield (R4).

- A Battle Unit is on the same Battlefield as the Waypoint it visits (partial reference in R3, which omits the Battlefield ID - to make this work, we had to change the Waypoint identifier so that Battlefield ID was one of its components).

- A Battle Unit must visit at least one Waypoint (R3).

Unfortunately, no constraint ensures that a Battle Unit visits a contiguous sequence of Waypoints (a route).

Model 16.3 would allow the specification of a Battle Unit that jumps between unconnected Waypoints like this:

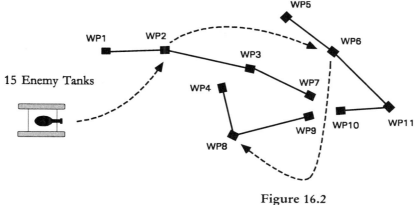

**Figure 16.2**

And that's definitely not what we want.

One way to constrain units to follow a route is to replace the VISITS 1:M relationship with a STARTS AT 1:1c relationship:

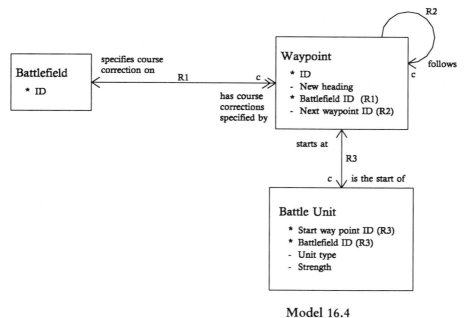

**Model 16.4**

By referencing only the point where the Battle Unit starts, relationship R2 can be accessed to find all the other Waypoints on the route. There is less to specify and, consequently, less potential for misspecification.

If we assume that a Battle Unit cannot be specified until its starting Waypoint is created, we can dispense with relationship R4 from Model 16.3.

Unfortunately, Model 16.4 allows a Battle Unit to start somewhere in the middle of a route like so:

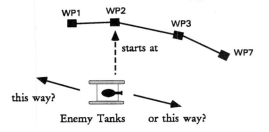

**Figure 16.3**

This is not good. A Battle Unit always starts at one end of a route and follows it all the way to the other end. We need to know the order in which all the Waypoints will be visited within a route.

**Adding the Route object**

We are getting into trouble because we have overlooked a critical object, Route, It should serve as a clue that an object is missing when a word central to the problem statement doesn't make its way into the model.

A Route is a connected sequence of Waypoints like this:

**Figure 16.4**

We want a Battle Unit to always move within a Route, so it makes sense to relate the Battle Unit object to the Route object instead of to the individual Waypoints. The Route object has other uses. We might, for example, want the ability to move and resize a Route, rather than moving all the Waypoints individually. Maybe we would even like to keep a library of Routes that can be loaded up like templates when planning a Battlefield mission. Actually, the best reason for modeling a Route may simply be that it exists.

The Route object is added to our information model below:

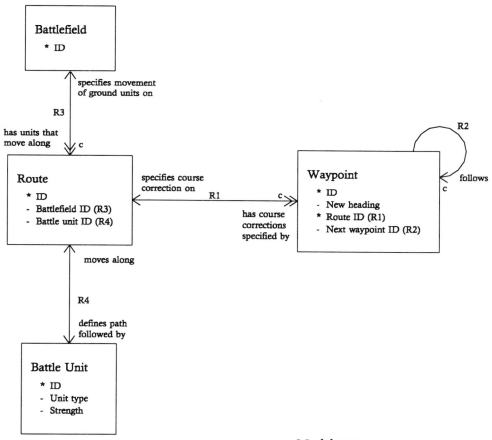

**Model 16.5**

A Battle Unit is assigned to an entire Route, but there is a problem with the definition of Route.

**Those unsightly gaps between Waypoints**

We would like to define Route as a completely connected set of one or more Waypoints. But since the FOLLOWS - R2 relationship is conditional, an unconnected Route like this could be specified,

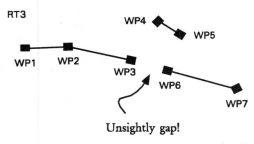

Figure 16.5

which we don't want.

**Closed Routes - another dead end**

We could try making the FOLLOWS - R2 relationship unconditional,

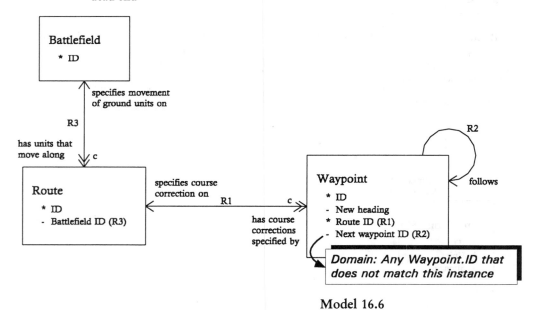

Model 16.6

but then all our Routes would have to be closed, like this...

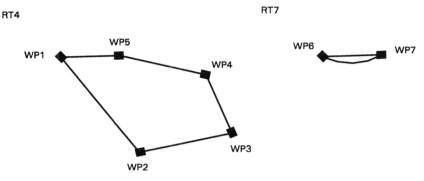

**Figure 16.6**

since every Waypoint would have to follow another Waypoint. Furthermore, the unconditionality of R2 would require that every Route contain at least two Waypoints: a starting Waypoint with a now mandatory following Waypoin, which cannot be the same Waypoint.

This is another example where twiddling the knobs and dials on the model takes us only so far. We need to stop model hacking and take another look at the problem.

**Taking another look**    Why is such a simple structure so difficult to model? Because,the associations among Waypoints in Route are not so simple. Here are some observations.

## Observations about Way Points in a Route

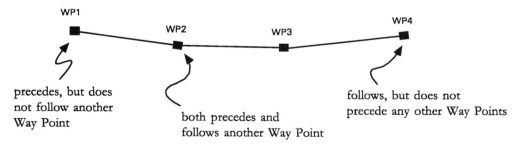

**Figure 16.7**

The way one Waypoint relates to another depends on whether a Waypoint is the start, middle or end of a Route. Subtyping should make it possible to differentiate these roles.

245

**Subtyping by position**   Here is a proposed subtyping with the observed relationships sketched informally.

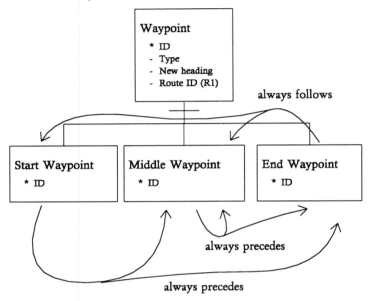

**Model 16.7**

We want to model the fact that a Start Waypoint must precede either a Middle Waypoint or an End Waypoint. A Middle Waypoint must precede either another Middle Waypoint or an End Waypoint, and so on. It is difficult to formalize the relationships due to all this "either" stuff. We need more certainty. We need to be using the word "always".

**Subtyping by referencing role**

Note that both Start and Middle Waypoints always PRECEDE and that both Middle and End Waypoints always FOLLOW. So maybe this is a better subtyping.

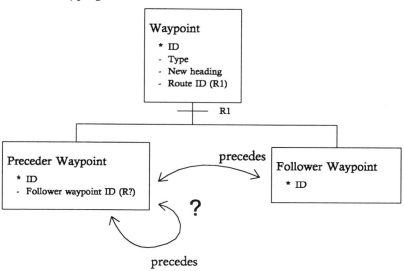

**Model 16.8**

**Subtyping both ways**

A Start Waypoint is always a Preceder. Good. An End Waypoint is always a follower. Good. A Middle Waypoint is both. Bad. But it is always both. Good!

Check this out.

**Model 16.9**

Model 16.9 says that every Waypoint is a Start, Middle or End Waypoint. Furthermore, each Start and Middle Waypoint PRECEDES a non-Start Waypoint. Non-Start Waypoint is synonymous with Follower Waypoint. Conversely, every Middle and End Waypoint IS PRECEDED BY a Non-End Waypoint (Preceder Waypoint). Notice that each Middle Waypoint serves both as a Preceder and as a Follower Waypoint.

Model 16.9 also addresses the problem of Route direction discussed earlier. A Route begins at a Start Waypoint. All the other Waypoints are related to a Route through relationships R6, R7 and R2.

It may be interesting to note that the self-referencing linear pattern in our application is now captured with a collection of nonreflexive relationships.

Does this interweaving of relationships look suspicious? You might feel that this supertype overlapping breaks the table formalism. So let's test it by trying to stuff this Route

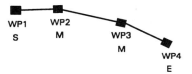

**Figure 16.8**

into these tables.

### Waypoint

WP1, S
WP2, M
WP3, M
WP4, E

| Start Waypoint | Middle Waypoint | End Waypoint |
|---|---|---|
| WP1 | WP2 | WP4 |
|  | WP3 |  |

| Preceder Waypoint | Follower Waypoint |
|---|---|
| WP1 -> WP2 | WP2 |
| WP2 -> WP3 | WP3 |
| WP3 -> WP4 | WP4 |

**Figure 16.9**

Notice that the Waypoint identifier values originate in the Waypoint object. The Waypoint.Type attribute has the domain [S | M | E] to differentiate Start, Middle and End Waypoint. The domain of the Preceder Waypoint identifier is formed by joining the Middle Waypoint.ID and the Start Waypoint.ID domains. For more information on forming subtype identifiers, see "Supertype identifier policies" on page 109.

What did we accomplish in this table exercise? We demonstrated that an example Route could be entered into the tables specified by our information model. Two questions remain:

1. Is it possible to enter illegal/malformed Routes into the tables?

2. Can we handle all the legal boundary conditions?

Let's address these questions in order.

**Precluding malformed Routes**    It would be nice if the following malformed routes were impossible to specify in our information model.

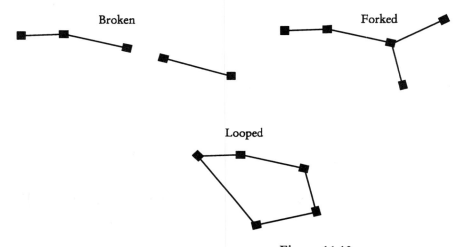

**Figure 16.10**

Forks are impossible because there are no one-to-many relationships in our model. Broken routes can't be specified because the PRECEDES relationship is unconditional. But what about the loop? Loops are not possible, again, because the PRECEDES - R2 relationship is unconditional. In fact, this

is the smallest legal Route. When a Waypoint is appended after WP2, WP2 changes into a Middle Waypoint, so the new Waypoint can be instantiated as an End Waypoint.

**The boundary condition - minimal Route**

This brings us to our second question, boundary conditions. It is impossible to have a Route with zero Waypoints since R4 is unconditional. But it should be possible to specify a single Waypoint Route:

Unfortunately, this case is illegal in Model 16.9. This minimal case will come in handy when we draw the first Waypoint of a Route! But how can we change the model to allow a single Waypoint in a Route? We can't make the PRECEDES - R2 relationship conditional because that would permit broken Routes and a few other bad things.

**The solution - adding a special case for the Start Waypoint**

A single Waypoint might be classified as a Start Waypoint since it represents the beginning of a Route. But a single Waypoint is not a Preceder Waypoint (yet).

We could create a special kind of Start Waypoint through subtyping, as shown.

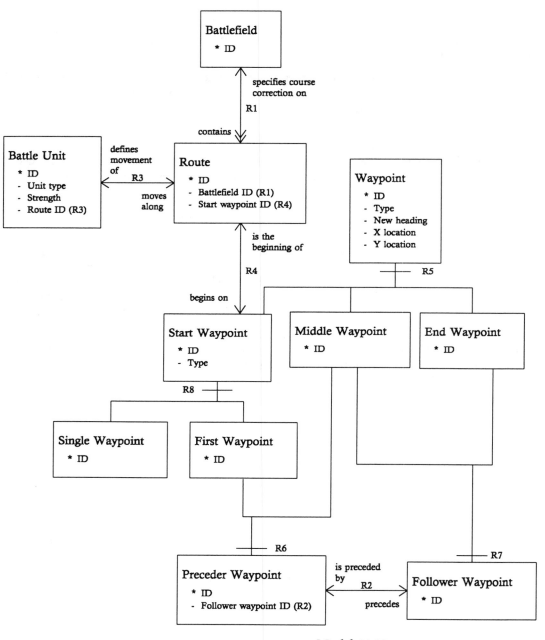

**Model 16.10**

Now we have two kinds of Start Waypoints - one that precedes and one that doesn't. Lesson: Putting a **c** on an arrow is only one way to handle a conditional relationship. In fact, throughout this exercise we have handled a problem replete with exceptions without the need for a single **c**!

**Mission editor summary**

So what are the important things to remember?

- You can model a sequence of points relationally.

- Even with a simple linear pattern, there can be a lot of rules to capture.

- If you capture these rules in an information model, it may take a lot of objects and relationships to get it right.

- A simple 1:1 or 1c:1c reflexive relationship may not suffice for every linear pattern.

- Overlapping supertypes can really come in handy.

**Which linear pattern model should you use?**

Model 16.10 is a more comprehensive statement of the mission editor application rules than any of its predecessors. But do we really want to use it? Good question. Models 16.9, 16.5 and 16.4 capture progressively less of the application, but they are simpler.

**The simpler the information model - the more complex the state model**

Any of these models can be made to work, but the number of application rules remains constant. So the less sophisticated the information model is, the more rules you must enforce in the state model actions. Actions are more difficult to debug and prove reliable than information model structures. Since the mission editor is an interactive game, a full set of edit operations must be supported. Consequently, the choice of Model 16.4 would leave quite a few actions and exceptions to be specified. So I would probably go whole hog and use Model 16.9 or 16.10. (Especially since I don't have to build them from scratch - I can just pull them out of my pattern library).

But let's say we were building a flight simulator that did not provide mission editing capabilities. Instead, the developers would supply a library of selectable missions. In that case, I would probably go with Model 16.4. Why? Because I would leave it up to the developers to make sure that they entered correct application data into the Battle Unit and Waypoint objects. Since the state models wouldn't enforce the entry of correct Routes, they wouldn't become complex.

**Early exposure argues for capturing as many rules as possible in the information model**

Visibility of application policy is another criteria. Model 16.10 exposes all the ugliness of the mission editor, so we see the full complexity of the application up front. This early exposure may inspire the analysts and the application experts to simplify or reinvent the application so it becomes less complex.

# Example 2: Polyline draw tool in an illustration program

Maybe you think the mission editor model could have been simpler if we had taken a different approach. Would the final model have been more straightforward if we tried to model a list of segments instead of a list of points? Let's find out!

In the mission editor exercise, we found that a linear structure looks unthreatening at a distance, but gets ugly when you grab it by the ears. This is because, relationship-wise, a linear pattern exhibits subtle complexity that you just don't appreciate until you get up close.

But sometimes a model is inordinately complex because you aren't thinking about it the right way. By recasting a problem's conceptual model you might end up with a less complex and more intuitive information model.

We modeled a sequence of Waypoints as connected vertices:

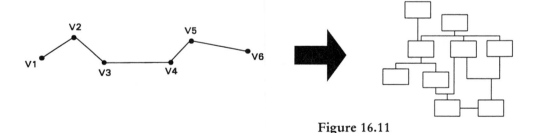

**Figure 16.11**

Would we get a less complex information model if we modeled a series of segments instead?:

**Figure 16.12**

For the mission planning editor application, the answer is no. This is because a single Waypoint was allowed, and a single Waypoint can't be modeled as a segment.

But a segment approach might work for the following problem. Consider a tool in an illustration program that can draw a polyline like this:

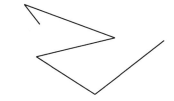

The smallest polyline possible consists of a single segment:

If someone starts to draw a line and doesn't finish

**Second point is not created**

then the initial point is deleted and nothing is drawn.

Let's start with this model:

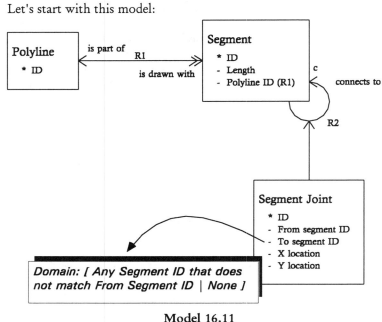

**Model 16.11**

This model says that:

- A Segment has length (Segment.Length).

- One Segment can be connected to another Segment (R2).

- The joint between two Segments is formed at an x,y location (Segment Joint.X,Y location).

- A Polyline must contain at least one Segment (R1).

- A Segment may not be joined to itself (domain description of To Segment ID).

But as you can see, making the x,y location attributes of the Segment Joint object leaves us without the start and end locations of a Polyline, as shown.

The position of Segment S2 is specified, but...

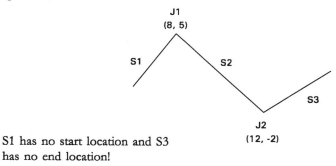

S1 has no start location and S3 has no end location!

**Figure 16.13**

Worse yet, if you have only one Segment, then there can be no Segment Joint and, consequently, no x,y locations at all!

We can fix this problem by attributing a start and end coordinate position to Segment instead.

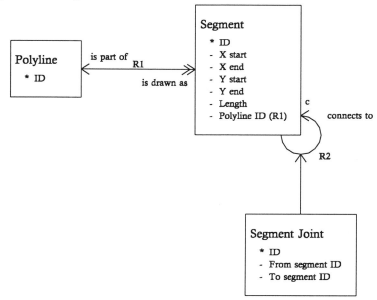

**Model 16.12**

Now we have a sequence of Segments with start and end points that is pretty good. Ideally, however, we would like to guarantee that the end x,y coordinate of one Segment coincides with the start x,y coordinate of the next Segment.

As it stands, Model 16.12 would allow specification of this set of supposedly connected Segments:

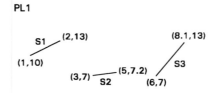

**Figure 16.14**

Fortunately, we can make the X, Y locations identifiers force the Segments to touch each other:

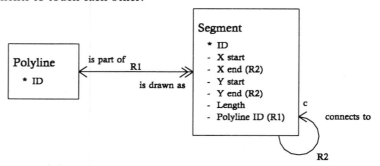

**Model 16.13**

We can now use the X, Y Start of the next segment as the X,Y End of the current Segment. The drawback to this approach is that the following case becomes illegal.

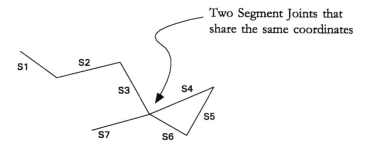

Figure 16.15

because you would end up with duplicate identifier values.

We just have to face it, there is no way to connect the end points of a Segment without modeling them as independent objects.

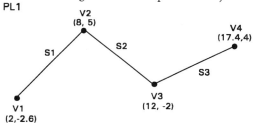

Figure 16.16

This leads us back to casting the problem as connected Vertices instead of connected segments, as we did with the mission editor solution (Model 16.9, with a few of the names changed).

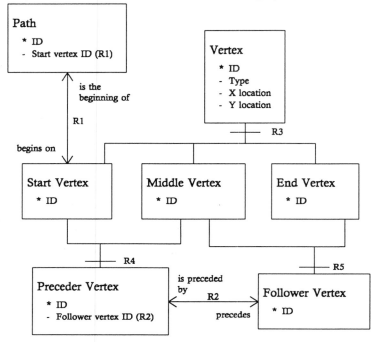

**Model 16.14**

We didn't use Model 16.10 because it permitted the existence of a lone Waypoint. A minimum of two Vertices is required in the Polyline application.

Conclusion

The original plan of modeling a Polyline as a relationship between Segments didn't get us too far. A better model was produced by modeling a Polyline as a relationship between Vertices. Consequently, the same pattern that worked in the mission editor application also works here.

# Summary

As you can see, linear patterns are more constrained than network patterns. It is important to study the rules of your application and ensure that they are precisely captured and exposed in your model.

# Chapter 17
# Tree patterns

So how exactly do you model a tree or hierarchical pattern with the Shlaer-Mellor method? This chapter explores an application that requires the analysis of a tree pattern. We are going to start off with a simple (one object, one relationship) information model. Then, step by step, we will identify limitations and devise improvements until we end up with a sophisticated information model that does a better job of capturing our application requirements. Even if you aren't especially interested in hierarchical structures, this modeling process will address more pragmatic modeling issues such as

> the degree to which application rules can be expressed in an information model and

> the degree to which application rules should be expressed in an information model,

just as we did in the previous chapter. Sound good? Great. Let's get to work! As always, we start off with a few words about our example application.

The purpose of this application is to keep track of a variety of auto-mobile parts (engines, pistons, doors, door handles, etc.) stored in a warehouse. The warehouse is owned and supplied by the AutoWare car company. The warehouse must service orders placed by mechanics and auto parts stores.

When there is a shortage of parts of a certain type, it may be necessary to obtain those parts by pulling them out of some other assembly. A door, for example, might be taken apart so that an order for a window crank can be filled.

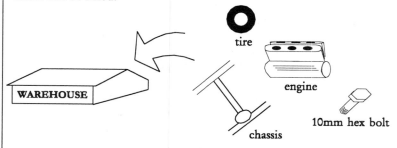

Not all the parts in the warehouse are manufactured by AutoWare. Some parts (usually things like bolts, gaskets, etc.) are bought from outside sources. These are stocked and shipped just like AutoWare parts. The only difference is that outside supplied parts are never disassembled.

For inventory and material control reasons, it is necessary to maintain a complete database of parts and part assemblies. It is not enough to know that an engine is in stock. It may be necessary to generate a complete list of all components in the engine down to the piston rings and bolts.

# A simple tree

**A simple tree of parts**

Here is an easy way to model the contents of the AutoWare warehouse:

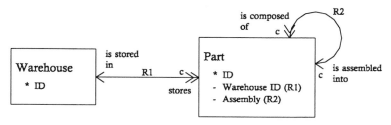

**Model 17.1**

Relationship R2 is a 1c:Mc reflexive relationship that organizes Parts into an assembly hierarchy.

This model says:

- A Part is always in a Warehouse (R1).

- A Part may be assembled from other Parts (R2).

    A bolt would be an example of a Part with no subparts.

- A Part may be assembled into one other Part (R2)

    This assumes that R2 really means "is a direct subassembly of," in which case the rule that "a Part can be built directly into no more than one other Part" is plausible. (This just highlights the importance of writing good relationship descriptions - See Chapter 12).

    What about the conditional case? A door is an example of a Part that is not assembled into any other Parts (assuming that it is intended to be shipped as a distinct unit). A spare bolt is also an example of a Part that is not built into anything.

- A Warehouse contains a bunch of Parts (R1).

    But it could be empty.

There is one application rule that Model 17.1 does not address. This becomes apparent when we consider specific instances of the Warehouse and Part objects.

**Problem: Part storage is sloppy**

Let's say that Part B is assembled into Part A. Obviously, if Part A is in Warehouse 3, then Part B must also be in Warehouse 3. But our simple model would let you say that Parts A and B are in different Warehouses! Or, put another way, Model 17.1 requires that you specify the Warehouse where each Part is located.

This is what our Parts tree looks like with Model 17.1:

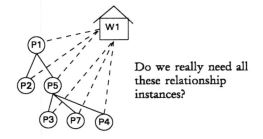

Do we really need all these relationship instances?

**Figure 17.1**

Figure 17.1 contains lots of superfluous relationship instances (dashed lines). We would prefer a model that (1) lets us specify the Warehouse containing a complete assembly and (2) forces us to infer that the constituent Parts are in the same location (a better reflection of reality).

## A tree with a root

A glance at Figure 17.1 suggests that we should relate Warehouse W1 to Part P1. To model this situation, we need to distinguish a complete assembly (the top of the tree) from an installed Part (the rest of the tree). Here is the idea.

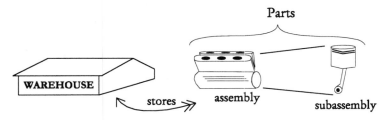

**Figure 17.2**

Then we can say that a complete Assembly is stored in a Warehouse and simply assume that the Parts built into the Assembly are at the same place.

**Only Assemblies are stored**    Here is the improved model.

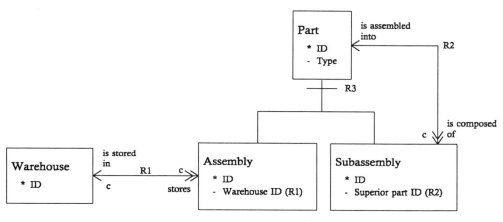

**Model 17.2**

To figure out where a Subassembly is stored, using Model 17.2, you must first find the encompassing Assembly using R2. This procedure eliminates the need to specify a relationship instance for every Part instance. Model 17.2 also precludes the possibility of specifying the physically impossible situation where an instance of Subassembly is stored in a Warehouse other than the one that stores the encompassing Assembly.

Here are the specific rules enforced in Model 17.2:

- A Part is either an Assembly or a Subassembly (R3).

- A Subassembly is *always* built into a Part that is either an Assembly or another Subassembly (R2).

- An Assembly, which is a Part, may or may not be built up from Subassemblies (this rule is given by the relationships R3➜R2).

- A Warehouse stores zero, one or many Assemblies.

There are two reasons why Relationship R2 is conditional on the many side: (1) A Part may be the lowest level Subassembly in an Assembly. (2) An Assembly may consist of only one Part and, thus, require no Subassemblies - a spare hubcap, for example.

Model 17.2 and Figure 17.2 are an elaboration of Model 17.1 and Figure 17.1. The subtyping of Part made it possible to single out Assembly for Warehouse storage and Subassemblies for building a Part hierarchy. By abstracting the Assembly object and pulling it out of the version of R2 in Model 17.1, we are assured that an Assembly is always at the top of any Part hierarchy.

If we populate Model 17.2 with the instances from Figure 17.1, our Parts tree now looks like this:

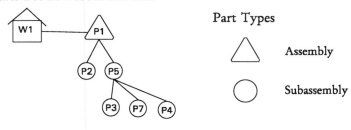

**Figure 17.3**

Model 17.2 is a definite improvement on Model 17.1, but it doesn't treat Parts that come from outside suppliers any different than proprietary Parts. Does that matter? According to the application note, non-AutoWare Parts are handled differently in at least two ways: (1) we have no visibility into the internal structure of a supplied part, and (2) supplied parts are supplied by a vendor.

# A tree with leaves

**Vendor supplied parts**    First let's take a look at a typical vendor supplied Part, a rubber seal, for example:

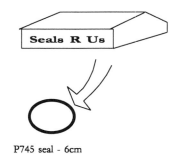

P745 seal - 6cm

**Figure 17.4**

For these kinds of Parts, we need to know the supplier/vendor information. Furthermore, we don't ever care about the components of a vendor supplied Part, even if it happens to be a complex assembly, because we would never disassemble and repackage it. Consequently, a supplied Part is never assembled from Subassemblies. The subtyping of Model 17.2 does not handle this case. How do we fix it?

We could extend our subtyping as shown,

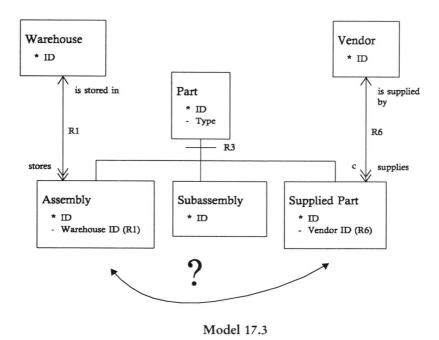

**Model 17.3**

but how does the IS COMPOSED OF Parts relationship (R2) fit in? Remember that we want to prevent a Supplied Part (or any type of Part for that matter) from being built into another Supplied Part.

To solve this problem I found it helpful to stare at some real examples instead of those tedious rectangles and arrows. So I drew several sketches. Here's a good one.

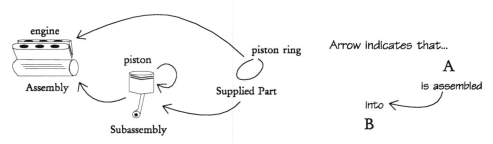

**Figure 17.5**

**Stealing and adapting the linear pattern**

Figure 17.5 shows that there is a reflexive relationship on Subassembly only. This looks a lot like the reflexive relationship sketched on Model 16.8. It's so similar, in fact, that I stole the whole linear pattern and adapted it to our hierarchical structure like this.

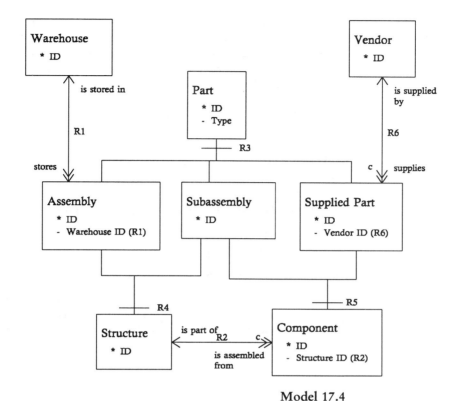

**Model 17.4**

You can see that the subtyping of Structure and Component in Model 17.4 is analogous to the subtyping of Preceder and Follower in Model 16.9. Also notice that, while the FOLLOWS relationship in the linear pattern is 1:1, the IS ASSEMBLED FROM relationship in Model 17.4 is 1:Mc. It makes sense that the only difference between a linear pattern and a tree pattern would be a change in the multiplicity of R2 from one to many. But is there some reason why our AutoWare application is conditional on R2 while the corresponding relationship in Model 16.9 is unconditional?

**A review of parts vocabulary**

Whether R2 should be conditional depends on our object definitions. Let's review them:

*Assembly:* A kit or fully built unit that is stored awaiting a shipping order. An engine would be an example of an Assembly if it was packaged as a kit or as a complete unit for sale. An engine built into a car, on the other hand, would be classified as a Subassembly.

*Subassembly*: A unit that is currently built into either an Assembly or a Subassembly. A piston Subassembly might be built into an engine Assembly, for example. If someone orders a piston individually and none is available as an Assembly, we might scavenge one from an engine, reclassify it as an Assembly and then ship it.

*Supplied Part*: A Part that a vendor has supplied. It has no internal structure as far as we are concerned.

Okay, now let's review some of the more interesting rules established in Model 17.4.

- Part is an Assembly, Subassembly or a Supplied Part.

- Assemblies and Subassemblies are Structures.

- Subassemblies and Supplied Parts are Components.

- A Component is always assembled into a Structure.

- A Structure is built up from zero, one or many Components (again, we allow for the case when we have a one-piece Assembly with no lower-level Components).

Let's populate our model with some example instances.

**Part Types**

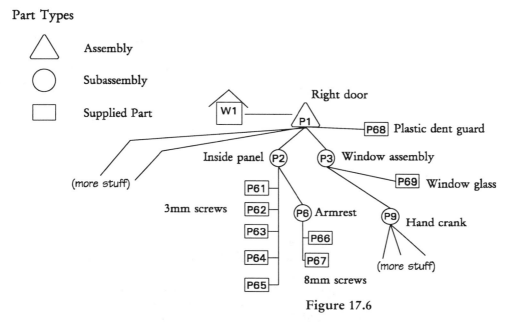

**Figure 17.6**

Figure 17.6 illustrates how we differentiate the root, leaves and intermediate nodes of our Parts tree. Our model accommodates the "Right Door" example just fine.

**Boundary cases**

We have at least two boundary cases to consider. First, can we handle an Assembly like "hubcap" that consists of only one Part? Yes. Since

R2 is conditional, we can define an Assembly that contains no lower level Parts.

Sketch of real-world entities: | Instances in the model:

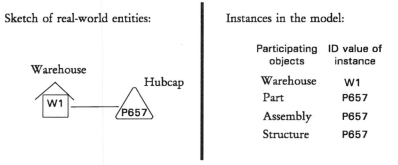

| Participating objects | ID value of instance |
|---|---|
| Warehouse | W1 |
| Part | P657 |
| Assembly | P657 |
| Structure | P657 |

**Figure 17.7**

Second, can we handle a Supplied Part that is not assembled into anything? AutoWare might buy a bolt from Bolt Barn that we simply resell as a spare part. Do we classify the bolt as an Assembly or a Component? We can make it an Assembly with no Components. Since R2 is conditional, that is no problem. Unfortunately, Model 17.4 wouldn't prevent me from saying that a Supplied Part, an engine let's say, broke down into Components. But that violates the application requirement that says we don't ever break down Supplied Components. The easiest solution might be to convince the application experts that this is a stupid requirement, but for the purposes of this exercise, let's say that we are stuck with the requirement. In that case, it would be nice to make Model 17.4 a little more bulletproof. Before doing that, can we just classify the bolt as a Component? We would have to change R2 to make it conditional on both sides, since Model 17.4 says that every Component must be built into a Structure.

**The danger of diluting object meanings**

Wait a minute - A Component that is *not* built into a Structure? And a Structure that is not made up of Components? Aren't we corrupting the whole idea of Structure and Component?

If we loosen up our semantic foundations, we are opening ourselves up to strange situations. We could end up with a Subassembly that isn't stored in a Warehouse.

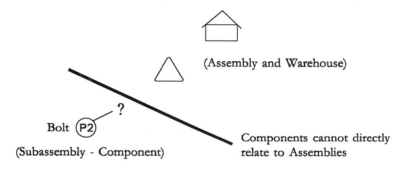

(Assembly and Warehouse)

Bolt (P2)

?

(Subassembly - Component)

Components cannot directly relate to Assemblies

**Figure 17.8**

**Better semantics**  We can increase the semantic integrity of our model by making R2 unconditional on both sides. To accommodate spare and supplied Parts, we need to change the way we subtype the leaves of our Parts tree. Here is one approach.

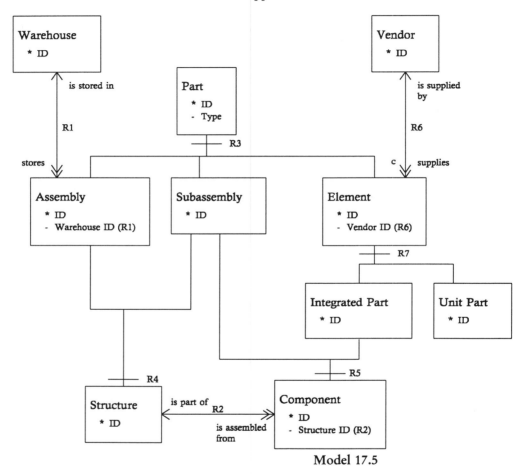

**Model 17.5**

The Supplied Part object from Model 17.4 has been replaced by the Element object in Model 17.5. An Element is a Part that cannot be broken down (by AutoWare) into subcomponents. This makes the subtyping on R3 more homogenous. Each subtype represents a level of assembly. Just because a part is at the bottom level of assembly doesn't necessarily mean that it is vendor supplied. AutoWare might stamp a special type of brace or hinge out of sheet metal, which can't be broken down.

**When is and when isn't a Part in an Assembly?**

To ensure that all elements clearly fall into one or the other of its subtypes, I chose the names Integrated and Unit Part. Unit Part takes the place of what I've been referring to as a spare part. In other words, an Element is either a Part that is integrated into the bottom level of an Assembly or it is a totally separate unit that cannot be further broken down.

**What does a Warehouse really store?**

There is one problem, however. We managed to leave Unit Parts completely out of the Warehouse! A Unit Part is an Element that is not a Component. We say that a Warehouse stores Assemblies, but a Unit Part is not integrated into an Assembly. We would like to draw another relationship between Warehouse and Unit Part, but having two such relationships can lead to relationship dependency[1] conflicts. No, what we really need to do is redefine what exactly it is that a Warehouse stores.

Let's focus on the kinds of things that the Warehouse can ship and draw another sketch.

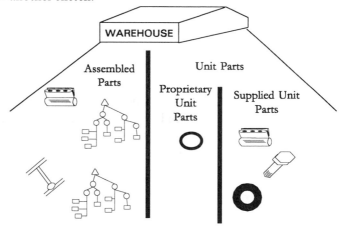

**Figure 17.9**

The nice thing about this sketch is that it both identifies all items that a Warehouse contains and it designates those objects that must have a direct relationship to the Warehouse object.

---

[1] S. Shlaer and S. Mellor, OOA: Domains and Objects (course notes), Project Technology, Inc., 1994, Chapter 6, Section 8 - Loops of Relationships.

Now let's take the perspective of a Vendor.

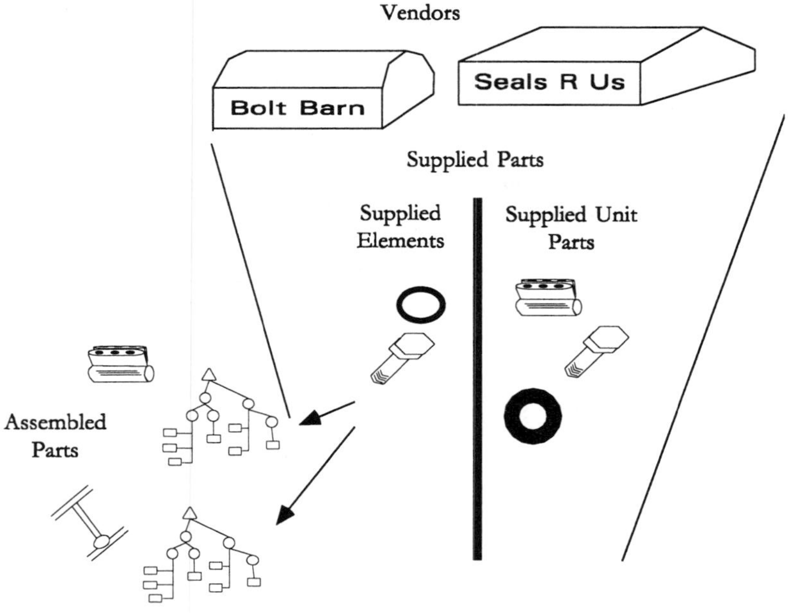

**Figure 17.10**

With the sketch in Figure 17.10, we establish that every vendor supplied Part is either an Element integrated into an AutoWare Assembly or a separately sold unit.

**The finished product**    Putting it all together we end up with this model.

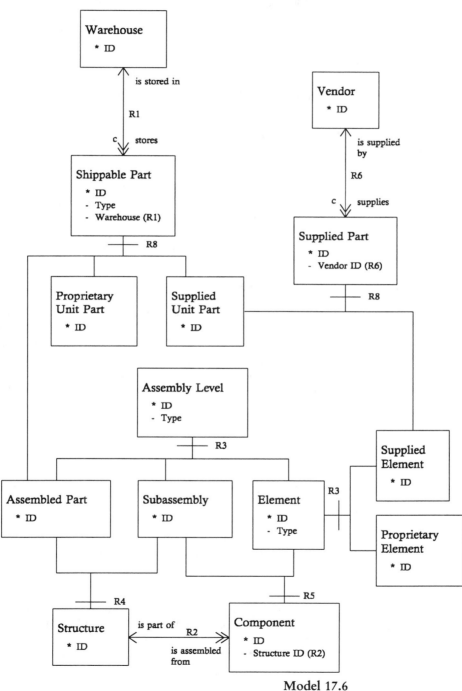

Model 17.6

**So what?**  After looking at Model 17.6, your first thought might be, "Why are there so many objects?" or maybe, "Jeez - there are a lot of subtypes!" Hold that thought for a moment while we consider some of the application rules integrated into our latest model.

- An Element is either supplied or proprietary.

- A Shippable Part is either fully assembled or it is a Proprietary or Supplied Unit Part.

- A minimal Assembled Part consists of at least two Assembly Levels: the top of the parts tree ( Assembled Part) and the bottom (Element).

The nice thing about Model 17.6 is that it captures so many application rules - not in algorithms, not in state model actions, but directly in the information model structure. The dynamic models built on Model 17.6 will have to handle fewer exceptions than dynamic models built on our earlier information model attempts.

# How much modeling is too much?

So what's the best choice, Model 17.1 or Model 17.6? Working with nothing more than the application description at the beginning of this chapter, there is no way to tell. I can say with certainty that Model 17.6 captures the application rules more thoroughly and more precisely than Model 17.1. I can also say that the state models built on Model 17.6 will be much less complex than those built on Model 17.1. Beyond that, you must consider your current degree of modeling skill and the needs of the project to make a good decision. Here are some things to consider:

- How important is it to verify that the informal application description is accurate? The author of Model 17.6 has a much better understanding of the application than someone who stops at Model 17.1.

- Have you solved a similar problem before? Is there an existing information model pattern that you can borrow and adapt? If so, it won't take long to knock out Model 17.6, so you might as well do it.

- To what degree has the rest of the application (neighboring subsystems) been modeled? Maybe you should build Model 17.1, model the neighboring subsystems, and then come back to Model 17.1 and extend it later. With the context of the rest of the application established, you may realize that Model 17.1 isn't so important in early versions or releases of the system that you are building. Then again, you may find that the subject matter covered by Model 17.1 is more central than you thought, leading you to build Model 17.6.

- If you lack Shlaer-Mellor modeling skill, it may take a considerable amount of time to produce Model 17.6. Are you more concerned about finishing the information modeling, even at the risk of missing some important issues, or are you more concerned about developing modeling skill?

- How much time do you have? That's easy - not enough! In my experience, a decision to skimp on the information model so that you can quickly get to the state and process models is usually a bad decision when it comes to saving time.

**Make a decision, move on and learn from it**

Having considered these factors, don't feel bad if you still aren't sure which approach is best. My advice is this: just make a decision - right or wrong - and forge ahead. What's the worst that can happen? If you build Model 17.1 and it turns out to be a mistake, you will find out somewhere in the middle of the state models. If the state models seem excessively complex because they handle too many application-related special cases and weird exceptions, then go back and fix the information model! On the other hand, if you build Model 17.6 and it turns out that the state models are too awkward because they perform a lot of overhead functions (managing unnecessary object and relationship instances) that have little to do with the application policies, then go back and simplify the information model. Ultimately, that's the only way to learn how thorough you should be when you build information models.

# Summary

In this chapter we modeled a tree pattern in an auto parts inventory application. We started out with a quick and dirty solution. This model was successively improved as we integrated more of the application requirements and exposed our model's limitations. We could see similarities between our tree model and the linear graph model we produced in Chapter 16. We finally arrived at a strong and extendible model that captured all the stated requirements.

# Index

# A

# B

# C

# D

# E

# F

# G

# H

# I

# K

# L

# M

# N

# O

# P

# Q

# R

# U

# V

# W